P9-BXY-658

Environment and Resource Policies
for the World Economy

Integrating National Economies: Promise and Pitfalls

Barry Bosworth (Brookings Institution) and Gur Ofer (Hebrew University)
Reforming Planned Economies in an Integrating World Economy

Ralph C. Bryant (Brookings Institution)
International Coordination of National Stabilization Policies

Susan M. Collins (Brookings Institution/Georgetown University)
Distributive Issues: A Constraint on Global Integration

Richard N. Cooper (Harvard University)
Environment and Resource Policies for the World Economy

Ronald G. Ehrenberg (Cornell University)
Labor Markets and Integrating National Economies

Barry Eichengreen (University of California, Berkeley)
International Monetary Arrangements for the 21st Century

Mitsuhiro Fukao (Bank of Japan)
Financial Integration, Corporate Governance, and the Performance of Multinational Companies

Stephan Haggard (University of California, San Diego)
Developing Nations and the Politics of Global Integration

Richard J. Herring (University of Pennsylvania) and Robert E. Litan (Department of Justice/Brookings Institution)
Financial Regulation in the Global Economy

Miles Kahler (University of California, San Diego)
International Institutions and the Political Economy of Integration

Anne O. Krueger (Stanford University)
Trade Policies and Developing Nations

Robert Z. Lawrence (Harvard University)
Regionalism, Multilateralism, and Deeper Integration

Sylvia Ostry (University of Toronto) and Richard R. Nelson (Columbia University)
Techno-Nationalism and Techno-Globalism: Conflict and Cooperation

Robert L. Paarlberg (Wellesley College/Harvard University)
Leadership Abroad Begins at Home: U.S. Foreign Economic Policy after the Cold War

Peter Rutland (Wesleyan University)
Russia, Eurasia, and the Global Economy

F. M. Scherer (Harvard University)
Competition Policies for an Integrated World Economy

Susan L. Shirk (University of California, San Diego)
How China Opened Its Door: The Political Success of the PRC's Foreign Trade and Investment Reforms

Alan O. Sykes (University of Chicago)
Product Standards for Internationally Integrated Goods Markets

Akihiko Tanaka (Institute of Oriental Culture, University of Tokyo)
The Politics of Deeper Integration: National Attitudes and Policies in Japan

Vito Tanzi (International Monetary Fund)
Taxation in an Integrating World

William Wallace (St. Antony's College, Oxford University)
Regional Integration: The West European Experience

Richard N. Cooper

Environment and Resource Policies for the World Economy

THE BROOKINGS INSTITUTION
Washington, D.C.

Copyright © 1994
THE BROOKINGS INSTITUTION
1775 Massachusetts Avenue, N. W., Washington, D.C. 20036

All rights reserved

Library of Congress Cataloging-in-Publication data:
Cooper, Richard N.
Environment and resource policies for the world economy/Richard N. Cooper
p. cm. — (Integrating national economies)
Includes bibliographical references and index.
ISBN 0-8157-1546-3 — ISBN 0-8157-1545-5 (pbk)
1. Environmental policy. 2. Natural resources.
I. Title. II. Series.
GE170.C66   1994
363.7—dc20   94-30855
                                                              CIP
                                                              r94

9 8 7 6 5 4 3 2 1

The paper used in this publication meets the minimum requirements of
American National Standard for Information Sciences—Permanence of Paper
for Printed Library Materials, ANSI Z39.48-1984

Typeset in Plantin

Composition by Princeton Editorial Associates
Princeton, New Jersey

Printed by R. R. Donnelley and Sons Co.
Harrisonburg, Virginia

ⓑ THE BROOKINGS INSTITUTION

The Brookings Institution is an independent organization devoted to nonpartisan research, education, and publication in economics, government, foreign policy, and the social sciences generally. Its principal purposes are to aid in the development of sound public policies and to promote public understanding of issues of national importance.

The Institution was founded on December 8, 1927, to merge the activities of the Institute for Government Research, founded in 1916, the Institute of Economics, founded in 1922, and the Robert Brookings Graduate School of Economics and Government, founded in 1924.

The Board of Trustees is responsible for the general administration of the Institution, while the immediate direction of the policies, program, and staff is vested in the President, assisted by an advisory committee of the officers and staff. The by-laws of the Institution state: "It is the function of the Trustees to make possible the conduct of scientific research, and publication, under the most favorable conditions, and to safeguard the independence of the research staff in the pursuit of their studies and in the publication of the results of such studies. It is not a part of their function to determine, control, or influence the conduct of particular investigations or the conclusions reached."

The President bears final responsibility for the decision to publish a manuscript as a Brookings book. In reaching his judgment on the competence, accuracy, and objectivity of each study, the President is advised by the director of the appropriate research program and weighs the views of a panel of expert outside readers who report to him in confidence on the quality of the work. Publication of a work signifies that it is deemed a competent treatment worthy of public consideration but does not imply endorsement of conclusions or recommendations.

The Institution maintains its position of neutrality on issues of public policy in order to safeguard the intellectual freedom of the staff. Hence interpretations or conclusions in Brookings publications should be understood to be solely those of the authors and should not be attributed to the Institution, to its trustees, officers, or other staff members, or to the organizations that support its research.

Board of Trustees

James A. Johnson
Chairman

Leonard Abramson
Ronald J. Arnault
Rex J. Bates
A. W. Clausen
John L. Clendenin
D. Ronald Daniel
Walter Y. Elisha
Stephen Friedman

William H. Gray III
Vartan Gregorian
Teresa Heinz
Samuel Hellman
Warren Hellman
Thomas W. Jones
Vernon E. Jordan, Jr.
James A. Joseph
Breene M. Kerr
Thomas G. Labrecque
Donald F. McHenry

Bruce K. MacLaury
David O. Maxwell
Constance Berry Newman
Maconda Brown O'Connor
Samuel Pisar
David Rockefeller, Jr.
Michael P. Schulhof
Robert H. Smith
John D. Zeglis
Ezra K. Zilkha

Honorary Trustees

Elizabeth E. Bailey
Vincent M. Barnett, Jr.
Barton M. Biggs
Louis W. Cabot
Edward W. Carter
Frank T. Cary
William T. Coleman, Jr.
Kenneth W. Dam
Bruce B. Dayton
Douglas Dillon
Charles W. Duncan, Jr.
Robert F. Erburu

Robert D. Haas
Andrew Heiskell
Roger W. Heyns
Roy M. Huffington
Nannerl O. Keohane
James T. Lynn
William McC. Martin, Jr.
Robert S. McNamara
Mary Patterson McPherson
Arjay Miller
Donald S. Perkins

J. Woodward Redmond
Charles W. Robinson
James D. Robinson III
Howard D. Samuel
B. Francis Saul II
Ralph S. Saul
Henry B. Schacht
Robert Brookings Smith
Morris Tanenbaum
John C. Whitehead
James D. Wolfensohn

Foreword

*T*HIS short book offers a conceptual framework for the international community as it assesses what to do about the environmental impact of economic activity and the use of natural resources. It accepts the current organization of the world into nation-states, which are sovereign over their respective territories. Under these circumstances, the author argues, exploitation of natural resources can properly be determined by national policy and market developments. The world need not be concerned about long-term shortages of resources, since price increases combined with technological advances deal satisfactorily with emerging scarcities, provided they emerge gradually.

Where resources are not subject to national jurisdiction, as in the cases of the open oceans, Antarctica, and even outer space, too rapid and uneconomic exploitation is likely; international regimes for management of the global commons are required, and indeed are being developed.

Economic activity is often damaging to the environment, especially to air and water quality. Where this damage is strictly local and where the local residents have adequate mechanisms for making their voices known in political decisions, antipollution actions should be left to national or subnational governments. In particular, the author suggests, it is not desirable for countries with stiff environmental protection to restrict imports from countries with lower requirements for environmental protection.

Some environmental impacts are global in character: ozone depletion and global warming are two examples. Here global action is necessary and appropriate, and mechanisms are required to discipline recalcitrant nations. But disagreements over priorities are likely, especially when outcomes are uncertain and proposed remedies are costly. In particular, developing countries are not likely to take actions to retard carbon emissions if those actions risk slowing their economic growth. Developed countries will have to proceed on their own in the near future or buy the cooperation of poor countries.

Richard N. Cooper is Maurits C. Boas Professor of International Economics at Harvard University and is associated with its Center for International Affairs. He is grateful to Kym Anderson, Ralph Bryant, Ann Hollick, Odile Roussel, Robert Solow, John Whalley, several State Department officials, and participants in a Brookings review conference in January 1994 for information, constructive criticisms, and suggestions. Kirsten Landers ably provided research assistance, and Beth Hastie helped in numerous ways with the evolving text. Rozlyn Coleman edited the final manuscript, and David Bearce verified its factual content.

Funding for the project came from the Center for Global Partnership of the Japan Foundation, the Curry Foundation, the Ford Foundation, the Korea Foundation, the Tokyo Club Foundation for Global Studies, the United States-Japan Foundation, and the Alex C. Walker Educational and Charitable Foundation. The author and Brookings are grateful for their support.

The views expressed in this book are those of the author and should not be ascribed to any of the persons or organizations acknowledged above, or to the trustees, officers, or staff members of the Brookings Institution.

BRUCE K. MACLAURY
President

September 1994
Washington, D.C.

Contents

Preface to the Studies on Integrating National Economies

E CONOMIC interdependence among nations has increased sharply in the past half century. For example, while the value of total production of industrial countries increased at a rate of about 9 percent a year on average between 1964 and 1992, the value of the exports of those nations grew at an average rate of 12 percent, and lending and borrowing across national borders through banks surged upward even more rapidly at 23 percent a year. This international economic interdependence has contributed to significantly improved standards of living for most countries. Continuing international economic integration holds out the promise of further benefits. Yet the increasing sensitivity of national economies to events and policies originating abroad creates dilemmas and pitfalls if national policies and international cooperation are poorly managed.

The Brookings Project on Integrating National Economies, of which this study is a component, focuses on the interplay between two fundamental facts about the world at the end of the twentieth century. First, the world will continue for the foreseeable future to be organized politically into nation-states with sovereign governments. Second, increasing economic integration among nations will continue to erode differences among national economies and undermine the autonomy of national governments. The project explores the opportunities and tensions arising from these two facts.

Scholars from a variety of disciplines have produced twenty-one studies for the first phase of the project. Each study examines the heightened competition between national political sovereignty and

increased cross-border economic integration. This preface identi-
fies background themes and issues common to all the studies and
provides a brief overview of the project as a whole.[1]

Increasing World Economic Integration

Two underlying sets of causes have led nations to become more
closely intertwined. First, technological, social, and cultural changes
have sharply reduced the effective economic distances among
nations. Second, many of the government policies that traditionally inhibited cross-border transactions have been relaxed or even
dismantled.

The same improvements in transportation and communications
technology that make it much easier and cheaper for companies in
New York to ship goods to California, for residents of Strasbourg
to visit relatives in Marseilles, and for investors in Hokkaido to buy
and sell shares on the Tokyo Stock Exchange facilitate trade,
migration, and capital movements spanning nations and conti-
nents. The sharply reduced costs of moving goods, money, people,
and information underlie the profound economic truth that technology has made the world markedly smaller.

New communications technology has been especially significant
for financial activity. Computers, switching devices, and telecommunications satellites have slashed the cost of transmitting information internationally, of confirming transactions, and of paying
for transactions. In the 1950s, for example, foreign exchange could
be bought and sold only during conventional business hours in the
initiating party's time zone. Such transactions can now be carried
out instantaneously twenty-four hours a day. Large banks pass the
management of their worldwide foreign-exchange positions
around the globe from one branch to another, staying continuously ahead of the setting sun.

Such technological innovations have increased the knowledge of
potentially profitable international exchanges and of economic op-

1. A complete list of authors and study titles is included at the beginning of this volume,
facing the title page.

portunities abroad. Those developments, in turn, have changed consumers' and producers' tastes. Foreign goods, foreign vacations, foreign financial investments—virtually anything from other nations—have lost some of their exotic character.

Although technological change permits increased contact among nations, it would not have produced such dramatic effects if it had been countermanded by government policies. Governments have traditionally taxed goods moving in international trade, directly restricted imports and subsidized exports, and tried to limit international capital movements. Those policies erected "separation fences" at the borders of nations. From the perspective of private sector agents, separation fences imposed extra costs on cross-border transactions. They reduced trade and, in some cases, eliminated it. During the 1930s governments used such policies with particular zeal, a practice now believed to have deepened and lengthened the Great Depression.

After World War II, most national governments began—sometimes unilaterally, more often collaboratively—to lower their separation fences, to make them more permeable, or sometimes even to tear down parts of them. The multilateral negotiations under the auspices of the General Agreement on Trade and Tariffs (GATT)—for example, the Kennedy Round in the 1960s, the Tokyo Round in the 1970s, and most recently the protracted negotiations of the Uruguay Round, formally signed only in April 1994—stand out as the most prominent examples of fence lowering for trade in goods. Though contentious and marked by many compromises, the GATT negotiations are responsible for sharp reductions in at-the-border restrictions on trade in goods and services. After the mid-1980s a large number of developing countries moved unilaterally to reduce border barriers and to pursue outwardly oriented policies.

The lowering of fences for financial transactions began later and was less dramatic. Nonetheless, by the 1990s government restrictions on capital flows, especially among the industrial countries, were much less important and widespread than at the end of World War II and in the 1950s.

By shrinking the economic distances among nations, changes in technology would have progressively integrated the world economy even in the absence of reductions in governments' separation fences. Reductions in separation fences would have enhanced interdependence even without the technological innovations. Together, these two sets of evolutionary changes have reinforced each other and strikingly transformed the world economy.

Changes in the Government of Nations

Simultaneously with the transformation of the global economy, major changes have occurred in the world's political structure. First, the number of governmental decisionmaking units in the world has expanded markedly and political power has been diffused more broadly among them. Rising nationalism and, in some areas, heightened ethnic tensions have accompanied that increasing political pluralism.

The history of membership in international organizations documents the sharp growth in the number of independent states. For example, only 44 nations participated in the Bretton Woods conference of July 1944, which gave birth to the International Monetary Fund. But by the end of 1970, the IMF had 118 member nations. The number of members grew to 150 by the mid-1980s and to 178 by December 1993. Much of this growth reflects the collapse of colonial empires. Although many nations today are small and carry little individual weight in the global economy, their combined influence is considerable and their interests cannot be ignored as easily as they were in the past.

A second political trend, less visible but equally important, has been the gradual loss of the political and economic hegemony of the United States. Immediately after World War II, the United States by itself accounted for more than one-third of world production. By the early 1990s the U.S. share had fallen to about one-fifth. Concurrently, the political and economic influence of the European colonial powers continued to wane, and the economic significance of nations outside Europe and North America, such as Japan, Korea, Indonesia, China, Brazil, and Mexico, increased. A world in which economic power and influence are widely diffused has displaced a world in which one or a few nations effectively dominated international decision-making.

Turmoil and the prospect of fundamental change in the formerly centrally planned economies compose a third factor causing radical changes in world politics. During the era of central planning, governments in those nations tried to limit external influences on their economies. Now leaders in the formerly planned economies are trying to adopt reforms modeled on Western capitalist principles. To the extent that these efforts succeed, those nations will increase their economic involvement with the rest of the world. Political and economic alignments among the Western industrialized nations will be forced to adapt.

Governments and scholars have begun to assess these three trends, but their far-reaching ramifications will not be clear for decades.

Dilemmas for National Policies

Cross-border economic integration and national political sovereignty have increasingly come into conflict, leading to a growing mismatch between the economic and political structures of the world. The effective domains of economic markets have come to coincide less and less with national governmental jurisdictions.

When the separation fences at nations' borders were high, governments and citizens could sharply distinguish "international" from "domestic" policies. International policies dealt with at-the-border barriers, such as tariffs and quotas, or responded to events occurring abroad. In contrast, domestic policies were concerned with everything behind the nation's borders, such as competition and antitrust rules, corporate governance, product standards, worker safety, regulation and supervision of financial institutions, environmental protection, tax codes, and the government's budget. Domestic policies were regarded as matters about which nations were sovereign, to be determined by the preferences of the nation's citizens and its political institutions, without regard for effects on other nations.

As separation fences have been lowered and technological innovations have shrunk economic distances, a multitude of formerly neglected differences among nations' domestic policies have become exposed to international scrutiny. National governments and international negotiations must thus increasingly deal with "deeper"— behind-the-border—integration. For example, if country A permits companies to emit air and water pollutants whereas country B does not, companies that use pollution-generating methods of production will find it cheaper to produce in country A. Companies in country B that compete internationally with companies in country A are likely to complain that foreign competitors enjoy unfair advantages and to press for international pollution standards.

Deeper integration requires analysis of the economic and the political aspects of virtually all nonborder policies and practices. Such issues have already figured prominently in negotiations over the evolution of the European Community, over the Uruguay Round of GATT negotiations, over the North American Free Trade Agreement (NAFTA), and over the bilateral economic relationships between Japan and the United States. Future debates about behind-the-border policies will occur with increasing frequency and prove at least as complex and contentious as the past negotiations regarding at-the-border restrictions.

Tensions about deeper integration arise from three broad sources: cross-border spillovers, diminished national autonomy, and challenges to political sovereignty.

Cross-Border Spillovers

Some activities in one nation produce consequences that spill across borders and affect other nations. Illustrations of these spillovers abound. Given the impact of modern technology of banking and securities markets in creating interconnected networks, lax rules in one nation erode the ability of all other nations to enforce banking and securities rules and to deal with fraudulent transactions. Given the rapid diffusion of knowledge, science and technology policies in one nation generate knowledge that other nations can use without full payment. Labor market policies become matters of concern to other nations because workers migrate in search of work; policies in one nation can trigger migration that floods or starves labor markets elsewhere. When one nation dumps pollutants into the air or water that other nations breathe or drink, the matter goes beyond the unitary concern of the polluting nation and becomes a matter for international negotiation. Indeed, the hydrocarbons that are emitted into the atmosphere when individual nations burn coal for generating electricity contribute to global warming and are thereby a matter of concern for the entire world.

The tensions associated with cross-border spillovers can be especially vexing when national policies generate outcomes alleged to be competitively inequitable, as in the example in which country A permits companies to emit pollutants and country B does not. Or consider a situation in which country C requires commodities, whether produced at home or abroad, to meet certain design standards, justified for safety reasons. Foreign competitors may find it too expensive to meet these standards. In that event, the standards in C act very much like tariffs or quotas, effectively narrowing or even eliminating foreign competition for domestic producers. Citing examples of this sort, producers or governments in individual nations often complain that business is not conducted on a "level playing field." Typically, the complaining nation proposes that *other* nations adjust their policies to moderate or remove the competitive inequities.

Arguments for creating a level playing field are troublesome at best. International trade occurs precisely because of differences among nations—in resource endowments, labor skills, and consumer tastes. Nations specialize in producing goods and services in which they are relatively most efficient. In a fundamental sense, cross-border trade is valuable because the playing field is *not* level.

When David Ricardo first developed the theory of comparative advantage, he focused on differences among nations owing to climate or technology. But Ricardo could as easily have ascribed the productive differences to differing "social climates" as to physical or technological climates. Taking all "climatic" differences as given, the theory of comparative advantage argues that free trade among nations will maximize global welfare.

Taken to its logical extreme, the notion of leveling the playing field implies that nations should become homogeneous in all major respects. But that recommendation is unrealistic and even pernicious. Suppose country A decides that it is too poor to afford the costs of a clean environment, and will thus permit the production of goods that pollute local air and water supplies. Or suppose it concludes that it cannot afford stringent protections for worker safety. Country A will then argue that it is inappropriate for other nations to impute to country A the value they themselves place on a clean environment and safety standards (just as it would be inappropriate to impute the A valuations to the environment of other nations). The core of the idea of political sovereignty is to permit national residents to order their lives and property in accord with their own preferences.

Which perspective about differences among nations in behind-the-border policies is more compelling? Is country A merely exercising its national preferences and appropriately exploiting its comparative advantage in goods that are dirty or dangerous to produce? Or does a legitimate international problem exist that justifies pressure from other nations urging country A to accept changes in its policies (thus curbing its national sovereignty)? When national governments negotiate resolutions to such questions—trying to agree whether individual nations are legitimately exercising sovereign choices or, alternatively, engaging in behavior that is unfair or damaging to other nations—the dialogue is invariably contentious because the resolutions depend on the typically complex circumstances of the international spillovers and on the relative weights accorded to the interests of particular individuals and particular nations.

Diminished National Autonomy

As cross-border economic integration increases, governments experience greater difficulties in trying to control events within their borders. Those difficulties, summarized by the term *diminished autonomy*, are the second set of reasons why tensions arise from the competition between political sovereignty and economic integration.

For example, nations adjust monetary and fiscal policies to influence domestic inflation and employment. In setting these policies, smaller countries have always been somewhat constrained by foreign economic events and policies. Today, however, all nations are constrained, often severely. More than in the past, therefore, nations may be better able to achieve their economic goals if they work together collaboratively in adjusting their macroeconomic policies.

Diminished autonomy and cross-border spillovers can sometimes be allowed to persist without explicit international cooperation to deal with them. States in the United States adopt their own tax systems and set policies for assistance to poor single people without any formal cooperation or limitation. Market pressures operate to force a degree of de facto cooperation. If one state taxes corporations too heavily, it knows business will move elsewhere. (Those familiar with older debates about "fiscal federalism" within the United States and other nations will recognize the similarity between those issues and the emerging international debates about deeper integration of national economies.) Analogously, differences among nations in regulations, standards, policies, institutions, and even social and cultural preferences create economic incentives for a kind of arbitrage that erodes or eliminates the differences. Such pressures involve not only the conventional arbitrage that exploits price differentials (buying at one point in geographic space or time and selling at another) but also shifts in the location of production facilities and in the residence of factors of production.

In many other cases, however, cross-border spillovers, arbitrage pressures, and diminished effectiveness of national policies can produce unwanted consequences. In cases involving what economists call externalities (external economies and diseconomies), national governments may need to cooperate to promote mutual interests. For example, population growth, continued urbanization, and the more intensive exploitation of natural resources generate external diseconomies not only within but across national boundaries. External economies generated when benefits spill across national jurisdictions probably also increase in importance (for instance, the gains from basic research and from control of communicable diseases).

None of these situations is new, but technological change and the reduction of tariffs and quotas heighten their importance. When one nation produces goods (such as scientific research) or "bads" (such as pollution) that significantly affect other nations, individual governments acting sequentially and noncooperatively cannot deal effectively with the resulting issues. In the absence of explicit cooperation and political leadership, too few collective goods and too many collective bads will be supplied.

Challenges to Political Sovereignty

The pressures from cross-border economic integration sometimes even lead individuals or governments to challenge the core assumptions of national political sovereignty. Such challenges are a third source of tensions about deeper integration.

The existing world system of nation-states assumes that a nation's residents are free to follow their own values and to select their own political arrangements without interference from others. Similarly, property rights are allocated by nation. (The so-called global commons, such as outer space and the deep seabed, are the sole exceptions.) A nation is assumed to have the sovereign right to exploit its property in accordance with its own preferences and policies. Political sovereignty is thus analogous to the concept of consumer sovereignty (the presumption that the individual consumer best knows his or her own interests and should exercise them freely).

In times of war, some nations have had sovereignty wrested from them by force. In earlier eras, a handful of individuals or groups have questioned the premises of political sovereignty. With the profound increases in economic integration in recent decades, however, a larger number of individuals and groups—and occasionally even their national governments—have identified circumstances in which, it is claimed, some universal or international set of values should take precedence over the preferences or policies of particular nations.

Some groups seize on human-rights issues, for example, or what they deem to be egregiously inappropriate political arrangements in other nations. An especially prominent case occurred when citizens in many nations labeled the former apartheid policies of South Africa an affront to universal values and emphasized that the South African government was not legitimately representing the interests of a majority of South Africa's residents. Such views caused many national governments to apply economic sanctions against South Africa. Examples of value conflicts are not restricted to human rights, however. Groups focusing on environmental issues characterize tropical rain forests as the lungs of the world and the genetic repository for numerous species of plants and animals that are the heritage of all mankind. Such views lead Europeans, North Americans, or Japanese to challenge the timber-cutting policies of Brazilians and Indonesians. A recent controversy over tuna fishing with long drift nets that kill porpoises is yet another example. Environmentalists in the United States whose sensibilities were offended by the drowning of porpoises required U.S. boats at some additional expense to amend their fishing practices. The U.S. fishermen, complaining about imported tuna caught with less regard for porpoises, persuaded the U.S. government to ban such tuna imports (both direct imports from the countries in which the tuna is caught and indirect imports shipped via third countries). Mexico and Venezuela were the main countries affected by this ban; a GATT dispute panel sided with Mexico against the United States in the controversy, which further upset the U.S. environmental community.

A common feature of all such examples is the existence, real or alleged, of "psychological externalities" or "political failures." Those holding such views reject untrammeled political sovereignty for nation-states in deference to universal or non-national values. They wish to constrain the exercise of individual nations' sovereignties through international negotiations or, if necessary, by even stronger intervention.

The Management of International Convergence

In areas in which arbitrage pressures and cross-border spillovers are weak and psychological or political externalities are largely absent, national governments may encounter few problems with deeper integration. Diversity across nations may persist quite easily. But at the other extreme, arbitrage and spillovers in some areas may be so strong that they threaten to erode national diversity completely. Or psychological and political sensitivities may be asserted too powerfully to be ignored. Governments will then be confronted with serious tensions, and national policies and behaviors may eventually converge to common, worldwide patterns (for example, subject to internationally agreed norms or minimum standards). Eventual convergence across nations, if it occurs, could happen in a harmful way (national policies and practices being driven to a least common denominator with externalities ignored, in effect a "race to the bottom") or it could occur with mutually beneficial results ("survival of the fittest and the best").

Each study in this series addresses basic questions about the management of international convergence: if, when, and how national governments should intervene to try to influence the consequences of arbitrage pressures, cross-border spillovers, diminished autonomy, and the assertion of psychological or political externalities. A wide variety of responses is conceivable. We identify six, which should be regarded not as distinct categories but as ranges along a continuum.

National autonomy defines a situation at one end of the continuum in which national governments make decentralized decisions with little or no consultation and no explicit cooperation. This response represents political sovereignty at its strongest, undiluted by any international management of convergence.

Mutual recognition, like national autonomy, presumes decentralized decisions by national governments and relies on market competition to guide the process of international convergence. Mutual recognition, however, entails exchanges of information and consultations among governments to constrain the formation of national regulations and policies. As understood in discussions of economic integration within the European Community, moreover, mutual recognition entails an explicit acceptance by each member nation of the regulations, standards, and certification procedures of other members. For example, mutual recognition allows wine or liquor produced in any European Union country to be sold in all twelve member countries even if production standards in member countries differ. Doctors licensed in France are permitted to practice in

Germany, and vice versa, even if licensing procedures in the two countries differ.

Governments may agree on rules that restrict their freedom to set policy or that promote gradual convergence in the structure of policy. As international consultations and monitoring of compliance with such rules become more important, this situation can be described as *monitored decentralization*. The Group of Seven finance ministers meetings, supplemented by the IMF's surveillance over exchange rate and macroeconomic policies, illustrate this approach to management.

Coordination goes further than mutual recognition and monitored decentralization in acknowledging convergence pressures. It is also more ambitious in promoting intergovernmental cooperation to deal with them. Coordination involves jointly designed mutual adjustments of national policies. In clear-cut cases of coordination, bargaining occurs and governments agree to behave differently from the ways they would have behaved without the agreement. Examples include the World Health Organization's procedures for controlling communicable diseases and the 1987 Montreal Protocol (to a 1985 framework convention) for the protection of stratospheric ozone by reducing emissions of chlorofluorocarbons.

Explicit harmonization, which requires still higher levels of intergovernmental cooperation, may require agreement on regional standards or world standards. Explicit harmonization typically entails still greater departures from decentralization in decisionmaking and still further strengthening of international institutions. The 1988 agreement among major central banks to set minimum standards for the required capital positions of commercial banks (reached through the Committee on Banking Regulations and Supervisory Practices at the Bank for International Settlements) is an example of partially harmonized regulations.

At the opposite end of the spectrum from national autonomy lies *federalist mutual governance*, which implies continuous bargaining and joint, centralized decisionmaking. To make federalist mutual governance work would require greatly strengthened supranational institutions. This end of the management spectrum, now relevant only as an analytical benchmark, is a possible outcome that can be imagined for the middle or late decades of the twenty-first century, possibly even sooner for regional groupings like the European Union.

Overview of the Brookings Project

Despite their growing importance, the issues of deeper economic integration and its competition with national political sovereignty were largely neglected in the 1980s. In 1992 the Brookings Institution initiated its project on Integrating National Economies to direct attention to these important questions.

In studying this topic, Brookings sought and received the cooperation of some of the world's leading economists, political scientists, foreign-policy specialists, and government officials, representing all regions of the world. Although some functional areas require a special focus on European, Japanese, and North American perspectives, at all junctures the goal was to include, in addition, the perspectives of developing nations and the formerly centrally planned economies.

The first phase of the project commissioned the twenty-one scholarly studies listed at the beginning of the book. One or two lead discussants, typically residents of parts of the world other than the area where the author resides, were asked to comment on each study.

Authors enjoyed substantial freedom to design their individual studies, taking due account of the overall themes and goals of the project. The guidelines for the studies requested that at least some of the analysis be carried out with a non-normative perspective. In effect, authors were asked to develop a "baseline" of what might happen in the absence of changed policies or further international cooperation. For their normative analyses, authors were asked to start with an agnostic posture that did not prejudge the net benefits or costs resulting from integration. The project organizers themselves had no presumption about whether national diversity is better or worse than international convergence or about what the individual studies should conclude regarding the desirability of increased integration. On the contrary, each author was asked to address the trade-offs in his or her issue area between diversity and convergence and to locate the area, currently and prospectively, on the spectrum of international management possibilities running between national autonomy through mutual recognition to coordination and explicit harmonization.

HENRY J. AARON   SUSAN M. COLLINS
RALPH C. BRYANT   ROBERT Z. LAWRENCE

Chapter 1

Introduction

NATURAL resources and the environment are nature's endowment to man. But the questions of ownership and appropriate use—even that of definition—remain complicated and divisive. What is a "natural resource"? To whom do the Earth's riches belong—all of mankind, the nations in which those riches are found, or individuals? Under the existing international system of nation states, countries have elected national ownership, or individual ownership within a national system of property rights, with a few stipulated exceptions (the deep seabed, outer space, and Antarctica), with the last still in contention. This allocation is widely accepted with respect to natural resources, but some environmentalists have raised questions about this distribution of property rights with respect to some *global* environmental issues, such as the tropical rain forests as producers of oxygen and as habitats for numerous, potentially valuable species.

At a philosophical level as well, one could raise questions about the existing allocation of property rights around the globe. Why should a relatively small number of Arabs own most of the world's proven oil reserves, for example? Or why should South Africans own most of the world's known gold and diamond resources? Or why should Americans and Canadians own the agriculturally rich Great Plains? Should not these resources be treated as endowments available to all mankind, to be allocated by collective decision?

But the international community long ago settled on a system of national ownership for good practical reason: disputes over natural

1

resources have been a leading cause of war—as most recently illustrated by Iraq's claim to Kuwaiti oil fields, against which the international community reacted strongly and militarily.

The clearest testimony to widespread approval of national ownership occurred in the 1970s, when the international community faced directly the possibility of collective ownership and decisively rejected it in the areas of greatest economic value—offshore oil and coastal fisheries.[1] Instead, it proceeded to allocate one-fourth of the earth's surface to national economic control in the form of 200-mile exclusive economic zones (plus the continental shelf where it extends beyond 200 miles from the coast), with the approval of many environmentalists as well as oil firms and fishermen. Only the residual deep seabed was retained as collective property, the common heritage of mankind, along with outer space.

The principle of state sovereignty over natural resources was recently reaffirmed in the 1992 Framework Convention on Climate Change, which is discussed in greater detail below, and the preamble of that convention recalls that "States have . . . the sovereign right to exploit their own resources pursuant to their own environmental and developmental policies, and the responsibility to ensure that activities within their jurisdiction or control do not cause damage to the environment of other States or of areas beyond the limits of national jurisdiction."[2] To open the issue of national ownership with respect to the environment would open many other issues as well, raising fundamental questions about how mankind has organized itself to carry out individual and collective activities. That is beyond the scope of this book. Rather, the book addresses ways for states—with their control over resources and most aspects of the environment—to cooperate with one another to mutual advantage.

The book opens with a brief discussion of natural resources. It then distinguishes among three analytical categories regarding en-

1. President Nixon proposed in 1970 that offshore oil outside a 3–12 mile national jurisdiction be treated as common heritage, to be managed by each coastal state on behalf of the international community with royalties to be paid to the international community. Official reaction around the world ranged from cool to hostile.
2. International Energy Agency (1992, p. 158).

vironmental use: (i) resources open to general use by common agreement; (ii) national ownership that materially affects outsiders through the market only, sometimes giving rise to charges of "eco-dumping"; and (iii) national ownership that materially affects outsiders beyond the market framework (that is, with positive or negative externalities). In each of these cases, national actions may affect the sensibilities of others (psychological externalities). Such sensibilities have become politically important and need to be dealt with if only for this reason.

These are analytical categories; in reality, cases often cut across analytical boundaries. For example, some uses of common property also generate externalities. All of these analytical distinctions also arise for economic actions within countries. But the book focuses on transnational issues, their implications for relations among states, the possible need for international policy action, the forms that such action have taken or should take, and the forms such actions are likely to take in the future.

Chapter 2

Natural Resources

THE commonsense notion of a "natural resource" is severely restricted by its place in time; over the long term, the notion of a "natural resource" is not well defined. The advance of technology has steadily converted "waste" into valuable material and will continue to do so. In the 1880s, for example, the world community could extract copper (for the budding electrical industry) from ores that contained 5 percent copper. Today, a century later, we extract copper from ores that contain only 0.3 percent copper, one-seventeenth the earlier concentration, at a price relative to other goods and services that was lower in 1990 than it was in the late nineteenth century.

What was worthless material has become an economic resource. "Dirt" is a natural resource now that the tailings (waste) of some old mines are being worked for the third time. Similarly, Pennsylvania rock oil was considered a sticky pollutant of streams until Benjamin Silliman, a professor of chemistry at Yale College, discovered how to convert it into kerosene in the 1850s, thus laying the basis for the modern petroleum industry. A nuisance was thus converted into a highly sought natural resource. As William Nordhaus has shown, copper and petroleum are not exceptional: the real price of most natural resources has declined over the past century, including agricultural land in the United States.[1]

1. Nordhaus (1992, pp. 23–28).

4

Induced technical change confounds the Ricardian rising cost curve in the long run: emerging scarcity creates an incentive to avert the scarcity or to bypass it with substitutes. Copper in nature has become physically scarcer but economically more abundant over the past century because of great improvements in extractive techniques. Kerosene was developed as a substitute for the increasingly scarcer whale oil, as the right whale was being depleted in the north Atlantic under the pressure of increasing demand for illumination. (The same incentives pushed whaling into the southern hemisphere around the same time, a development made possible by better techniques for preservation.) Similar processes of induced technical change produced nylon as a substitute for silk around 1930 and more than doubled the fuel efficiency of aircraft engines between 1970 and 1990, a period that saw two sharp increases (and one subsequent decrease) in world oil prices.

The dominant innovation of modern economies in the late twentieth century is that the search for technical improvements has been institutionalized. Modern societies no longer rely on economic incentives to individuals to find better ways to accomplish old objectives. Full-time and salaried individuals at universities, research institutions, and the laboratories of major companies now search continuously for technical improvements, guided both by recent scientific developments and by economic incentives to firms and society as a whole. For this reason, "exhaustion" of natural resources should not be a concern in the very long run. Only two inputs are ultimately required to satisfy all man's material needs on earth: brainpower and energy. Since energy is one resource with respect to which the earth is not a closed system, receiving from the sun vast amounts daily, both inputs will be in ample supply if society manages its affairs sensibly.[2]

In the medium run, which represents the long run for most mortals, particular resources may become scarcer, but market

2. This optimistic view represents Nordhaus's (1992, pp. 29–31) counterfactual of a perfectly elastic supply schedule in the long run. Nordhaus is more cautious, allowing for resource and environmental "drag" on future economic growth; his more cautious approach reduces growth rates by 0.3 percent a year between 1980 and 2050, of which half is due to energy. Cumulated over 70 years, that reduction implies a gross domestic product 19 percent lower than otherwise.

mechanisms can generally handle well the emerging scarcities, encouraging conservation as well as the search for effective substitutes. Consider the example of fish, the price of which has risen in recent decades relative to other forms of animal protein, partly in response to higher demand for health reasons and partly in response to the depletion of stocks, which has raised the costs of fishing relative to those of raising poultry or beef. This price increase will discourage consumption and encourage production, including fish farming, which is growing rapidly. (Attempts to increase production in traditional fishing grounds will sharply raise the costs of fishing in those grounds because of stock externalities, thus creating a special problem of resource management.)[3]

Is this view consistent with the desirability of sustainable development? The Brundtland report of 1987 defined sustainable development as that which "meets the needs of the present without compromising the ability of future generations to meet their own needs."[4] With respect to extraction of natural resources, sustainable development is achieved if the rents on those resources are used for net investment at good available rates of return, a condition that has been well met in recent years.[5] For example, in 1992, world exports of all mineral products amounted to $444 billion, of which $331 billion were fuel exports (mostly oil). Generously estimated, world production was twice that, or something under $1 trillion.[6] Although 1992 was an economically weak year in the industrialized countries, net investment worldwide exceeded $1 trillion, not counting "soft" investments in education and research and development. So even if the whole $1 trillion is attributed to rents—that is, the costs of production are ignored—the Solow criterion (described in Robert Solow's 1992 paper) is comfortably satisfied. This rough calculation does not allow, however, for possible mismanagement today of renewable resources—depletion of

3. Stock externalities arise when several parties independently draw on the same common pool of resources. Extractions by one party increase the costs to all the others.

4. World Commission on Environment and Development (1987, p. 8).

5. See Solow (1992).

6. Figures on the export of mineral products are from General Agreement on Tariffs and Trade (1993, pp. 1, 2, 49).

forests, water tables, and arable soil—but their inclusion is not likely to overturn the main conclusion.

In the very short run of months or a few years, unexpected shortages of critical materials may cause extreme social disturbance. Petroleum and food grains come to mind. The solution for each nation, and for the world, is to diversify sources of supply and possibly to supplement diversification with storage. International action (concerted policy action by states) is not required, except for the financing and management of sufficient emergency stocks where desirable, such as the national oil stocks maintained by agreement under the auspices of the International Energy Agency (IEA) or the emergency food stocks encouraged (but not provided) under the World Food Program and the Food and Agriculture Organization (FAO).[7]

Preservation of the earth's biological diversity has been elevated to the international agenda and led in 1992 to the signing of a convention to preserve it. Some important differences among the major interests remain, however. One of these is that while most kinds of plants and animals reside in countries and are thus national "natural resources," some environmentalists argue that genetic material should be regarded as a common heritage of mankind, entitled to special protection because it provides the basis for continuing evolution.[8] Land-based natural genetic material can be bought in situ or stored elsewhere, however. Increasingly genes will be subject to artificial construction—new substances will be created to supplement or substitute for natural ones—so that genetic material, particularly within a few decades, will not be radically different from other resources. But protecting

7. The challenge for collective action here lies in the unity of the world market, combined with the fact that holding above-normal stocks is costly. A single nation holding stocks performs a global public service (even targeted release will lower prices for everyone in a period of shortage) for which it bears the full cost. Without coordination, stock-holding against possible contingencies may be suboptimal. The International Energy Agency (IEA) requires its 22 members to hold oil stocks equal to not less than 60 days' imports. The IEA also has arrangements for sharing limited supplies in an emergency, defined as a quantitative shortfall of at least 7 percent of imports in the preceding year. See Daniel B. Badger, Jr., "International Cooperation during Oil Supply Disruptions: The Role of the International Energy Agency," in Horwich and Weimer (1988, pp. 1–16).

8. Sidney Holt, "Towards Ensuring the Rights of Future Generations: Scientific Aspects," in Busuttil and others (1990, p. 111).

natural genetic material requires well-defined and secure property rights *within* countries, and genetic engineering is uncertain both as to extent and as to timing. These considerations lent worldwide support to an injunction in the 1992 Convention on Biological Diversity (article 8) that countries "as far as possible and as appropriate" establish protected areas, protect natural ecosystems from a variety of intrusions, and generally manage their affairs in ways that preserve biological diversity. The convention's preamble accepts national control over genetic material, reaffirming that "states have sovereign rights over their own biological resources," but the convention reflects an international interest in how states handle the material within their borders.

The Bush administration of the United States declined to sign the convention, but not because it disagreed with its objectives. Rather, U.S. objections concerned control over internationally arranged financing to pursue the objectives (article 21) and especially the requirement that governments in effect alter their systems of patent protection to transfer technology to the governments of developing countries on "most favorable" terms (article 16), issues that had arisen in previous North-South negotiations in which the United States also declined to agree (for example, the Draft Treaty on Law of the Sea).[9]

Preservation of biodiversity poses difficult questions for public policy, since it involves preserving future options of unknown future value. The world contains an estimated 33.5 million species of plants and animals, of which only 4 percent have been identified.[10] Nearly 90 percent of these total estimated species—or 30 million species—are insects, of which fewer than 800,000 have been identified. Under these circumstances, it is difficult to estimate the cost of losing 1,000 or even one million species through

9. Quotes of the convention are from Gardner (1992). See also Burk, Brovsky, and Monroy (1993). The Clinton administration in 1993 indicated that it would sign the biodiversity convention, subject to provision of adequate safeguards to intellectual property rights. Since the Bush administration failed in its attempt to negotiate satisfactory language on this issue, it is unclear how the Clinton Administration will achieve that aim, except perhaps in exchange for relaxing U.S. reservations on the financial provisions of the convention. Its first step was to attach a unilateral "understanding" to the convention that would become part of the Senate record.

10. World Bank (1992, p. 60).

extinction. Insofar as they are land-based species and subject to acquisition (most of them are in the tropics and highly localized), one is tempted to say they have no value beyond the aesthetic of knowing they exist, since if they had value above the cost of acquisition individuals or companies would have acquired them.[11] Possible value in the future is not sufficient to establish value in the present. Spent nuclear fuel contains abundant unused energy that may be of great value in the future but is accorded negative value today because of its toxicity. The ground under a building may have great future value, but as a rule its present value may reflect only its value as urban real estate, not as a potential future resource.

Some experts consider the existing array of species as priceless,[12] but it is difficult to sustain a view that high social cost should be paid to preserve *all* species, especially in tropical (highly speciated) countries with widespread poverty. Attempts even to measure diversity in a systematic way are in their infancy.[13] Much loss of species occurs when tropical forests are cut and the traditional ecology destroyed. This fact has drawn attention to trade in tropical timber, on which there has been international agreement since 1983 (renewed in 1994) that harvesting should be on a sustainable basis. But according to one estimate, 80 percent of the wood harvested in developing countries is used for fuel and charcoal, which is not regulated by international accord.[14] Clearing land for subsistence agriculture

11. Two developments suggest that unexplored genetic material may have some market value. In 1991, the pharmaceutical firm Merck paid $1.3 million to a private Costa Rican research institute to provide roughly 10,000 natural biological samples over the following two years. Merck would hold the patents on any marketable product that emerged from these samples but would pay a fair royalty to the Costa Rican institute, which, in turn, would share it with the government for the maintenance of national parks. Julia Preston, "A Biodiversity Pact with a Premium," *Washington Post*, June 9, 1992, A16.

Second, since 1987 there have been at least 17 "debt-for-nature" swaps, whereby private organizations have raised $16 million to buy about $100 million face value in developing country debt, which was subsequently canceled in exchange for arrangements by the debtor countries to expand their programs for preserving the natural environment. See World Bank (1992, p. 169).

12. See Wilson (1992), who has specialized in the study of insects.

13. Weitzman (1992).

14. Kym Anderson, "Effects on the Environment and Welfare of Liberalizing World Trade: The Cases of Coal and Food," in Anderson and Blackhurst (1992, p. 165).

is also an important factor in the loss of tropical forest. Economic development that alleviates poverty would therefore reduce destruction of tropical forests and the loss of species.

Building on earlier, more limited precedents, the international community in 1973 agreed on a Convention on International Trade in Endangered Species of Wild Flora and Fauna (CITES), which requires both import and export licenses for trade in any species that is threatened with extinction or that may become endangered under conditions of unregulated trade. Countries may also request international cooperation in controlling trade in species subject to regulation in their national jurisdiction. But this agreement does not cover species lost to ecological changes.

Some species migrate across national boundaries and are accessible to populations in more than one country, giving rise to possible overexploitation, as discussed in the next chapter. An earlier 1950 convention aims at protecting migratory birds from overexploitation and extinction.

Chapter 3

Common Heritage

COMMON heritage, as generally acknowledged in international law, includes the open oceans and their inhabitants, the deep seabed, outer space, and (more controversially) Antarctica. Except for the first, these domains are presently protected by the high cost of exploitation. But one can imagine that these cost barriers will fall over time, and eventually these domains will suffer the "tragedy of the commons:" excessively rapid and intense exploitation arising from the perverse incentives present in general access to a valued resource.[1] International conflicts will likely ensue.

Sooner or later a regime to preserve the resource is usually established. The 200-mile exclusive economic zone (EEZ) was an attempt to do this for near-coastal waters, although it has not worked out well, because national rights to the EEZ are not the same as exclusive property rights and because most countries have bungled their domestic management of the EEZ, allowing too easy access to nationals and to foreigners willing to pay a fee. In the United States, for instance, total employment in the fishing industry rose by 60 percent between 1970, prior to the EEZ, and 1988, yet the total catch in most U.S. fisheries remained roughly constant during the 1980s. Productivity (tonnage per worker) remained essentially unchanged over the two decades, despite great improvements in the technology of fishing, with regard to finding

1. The 1958 treaties on management of the oceans contain no suggestion on the possibility of exploiting the mineral resources of the seabed. Yet within 20 years that became one of the most contentious issues of the Law of the Sea Conference.

11

and catching fish.[2] As the EEZ forced out foreigners, U.S. fishermen took their place. Instead of using the occasion of reduced foreign fishing to rebuild stocks, U.S. policy encouraged increased fishing by Americans. Fisheries management in most other countries has been just as poor, or even worse, following the creation of EEZs.

Nascent international preservation regimes, involving stipulated prohibitions and rights of use, exist for Antarctica, outer space, and the deep seabed; there are also international regimes for limiting the harvest of some common property resources, such as seals and whales, and for allocating the electromagnetic spectrum. All these will be briefly described. The central issue, as the world community moves away from laissez faire, is the choice between partition (allocation of well-defined property rights) and joint management, and their possible combination.

Antarctica[3]

Antarctica and its resources are at an earlier stage of resource exploitation than the oceans, because of the region's difficult phys-ical environment and the complex political regime that governs Antarctica. The approach of the international community has been to respond to resource issues on a joint or cooperative basis, but with an emphasis on national enforcement and self-policing.

Arrangements for Antarctic resources are developed by a 25-member Antarctic Consultative Group. This institutional mecha-nism evolved from the political and scientific history of the area. The year 1957–58, the International Geophysical Year, included an Antarctic research phase. The 12 countries that participated in Antarctic scientific research included 7 states that claimed terri-tory in Antarctica (Argentina, Australia, Chile, France, New Zea-land, Norway, and the United Kingdom) and 5 countries that

2. Data on U.S. fishing are from Bureau of the Census (1992, p. 678). The major exception was the Alaskan pollack industry (nonexistent in 1980), in which growth ex-ceeded the increase in total U.S. output of fish but accounted for only a small portion of the growth in employment.

3. The next three sections draw heavily on Hollick and Cooper (1991). See also Waller (1989).

neither claimed nor recognized others' claims to territory (Belgium, Japan, South Africa, the United States, and the Soviet Union).

In 1959, the 12 researching governments institutionalized their cooperative scientific relationship in a treaty. The resulting Antarctic Treaty of 1961 applies to the area south of the 60-degree latitude. Territorial claims were set aside while research activities have been carried on. Research plans and scientific findings are freely exchanged. The area is to be used only for peaceful purposes and treaty-state observers have free access and inspection rights to all installations and equipment. The treaty further provides for peaceful dispute settlement and for an ongoing consultative mechanism.

Additional countries have been free to accede to the treaty, and 30 countries have chosen to do so since 1961. Of these new members, 14 became "consultative parties" by undertaking substantial scientific research in Antarctica: Poland (1977), the Federal Republic of Germany (1981), India and Brazil (1983), China and Uruguay (1985), German Democratic Republic and Italy (1987), Spain and Sweden (1988), Finland, Republic of Korea, and Peru (1989), and Ecuador and Netherlands (1990). Consultative parties are entitled to vote at biennial consultative meetings. Other states may participate in the discussions as observers and in meetings called to deal with resource issues. Consultative parties, however, enjoy special status as decisionmakers in the treaty system.

As resource questions have arisen, the consultative parties have handled them on a case-by-case basis. Two broad types of resources have been at issue—living and nonliving. The basic political issues have been those of claimants versus nonclaimants and, where claims overlap, claimants versus claimants. An important factor in overcoming these tensions within the consultative group has been the eagerness of other members of the United Nations to help manage Antarctica. The prospect of UN involvement has been an important incentive to maintaining the cohesion and the viability of the Antarctic consultative process. At the 1983 General Assembly, the United Nations first resolved to study the Antarctic issue and has since kept it on the agenda.

Antarctic resources became central concerns of the consultative parties early in the life of the treaty. In the 1960s, *living resources* were in the forefront. Nations had already grappled in the 1930s with how to regulate the harvest of Antarctic whales. The International Whaling Commission (IWC), set up in 1946, has restricted whaling on a global basis consistent with the dispersal and range of the resource. The consultative parties, however, have addressed only resources limited to Antarctica. In 1964, "Agreed Measures for Conservation of Antarctic Fauna and Flora" was adopted and in 1966 the "Interim Guide Lines for the Voluntary Regulation of Antarctic Pelagic Sealing" was adopted. The latter served as the basis for the 1972 Convention on the Conservation of Antarctic Seals (CCAS), which was negotiated in a larger framework that reflected the wide migratory range of seals.

By the late 1970s, the displacement of Soviet and Japanese distant water fleets from the newly claimed 200-mile zones was putting greater pressure on Antarctic living resources, in particular a small shrimp known as krill. In 1980, after difficult negotiations, the Antarctic Consultative Group concluded the Antarctic Living Marine Resources Agreement. The problem of how to deal with the seven territorial claimants was handled by expanding the resource management area to encompass an ecological unit known as the "convergence zone." This ecosystem contains all interrelated Antarctic species, and it contracts and expands with seasonal change. The zone is important from a political perspective, because it encompasses islands that are under recognized national jurisdiction, such as Kerguelen (France). Thus, it has been possible to develop a formula that avoids the issue of national claims to the Antarctic mainland by this device.

The treaty relies on data collection by participating states to keep all parties informed about the condition of the resource. When participating scientists agree that the data suggest the need to reduce fishing, consensual decisionmaking (whereby all parties must agree, or at least acquiesce) is required to effect a system of allocation. Not surprisingly, agreement on the scientific evidence, when that evidence can lead to decisions to reduce the harvest of a particular species, is difficult. The 1980 agreement lays the foundation for cooperative management. Groups have been set up under the Scientific Committee to collect and assess data on krill, fish, and ecosystems. A number of conservation measures have been taken, ranging from minimum mesh sizes, total allowable catch, and closed seasons for certain fisheries, to limits and even prohibitions on fishing certain species in designated areas. The consensual decisionmaking process has predictably slowed the process of adopting conservation measures. Given open access, however, there is no alternative to some form of consensus, and the linkage to a scientific research program has helped.

The *nonliving resources* of Antarctica, particularly offshore oil and gas, became the focus of attention in the 1980s following two major oil price increases. Little is known of the mineral potential of the continent, although Antarctica is suspected of containing minerals similar to those found in Australia, South Africa, and the Chilean-Argentine peninsula. In 1981, the Antarctic consultative parties committed themselves to negotiating a minerals regime for the continent.

By 1988, the consultative parties adopted by consensus the Convention on the Regulation of Antarctic Mineral Resource Activities (CRAMRA). Thirty-three states participated in the final meeting (20 consultative parties) and are eligible to ratify the treaty; ratification had not occurred by mid-1994. The convention covered three stages of mineral activity: prospecting, exploration, and development. Exploration and development activities were subject to prior authorization, but prospecting could be undertaken with advance notice and subject to regulations adopted by the commission. CRAMRA provided for the establishment of a plenary commission with general authority, regulatory committees (ten members each) to manage each of the geographic areas yet to be identified, and a scientific and environmental advisory committee to provide expert advice. As envisioned by the drafters, each committee would proceed in stages to (i) promulgate general requirements, (ii) review and approve applications, and (iii) monitor activities to ensure conformance with requirements set out by the commission.

CRAMRA was carefully crafted to take account of the different interests in Antarctica. To come into effect, 16 of the 20 consultative parties who were at the final negotiations must ratify the agreement. These states must include those needed for the regulatory commissions to function—the United States, the Soviet Union (now Russia), and the 7 claimants; they must also include 5 developing countries and 11 developed countries.

The treaty was designed neither to encourage nor discourage exploration and development. However, unlike the living resources convention, activities (except prospecting) are prohibited until decisions are taken to ensure that mineral activities will take an acceptable form. In particular, opening a specific area for exploration and development would require a consensus. Specific proposals would then be decided by qualified majorities. Environmental protection is an integral part of CRAMRA. An environmental impact assessment is among the requirements to initiate exploration, as is agreement on a liability protocol. A system of inspection and reporting is provided, as well as procedures for compulsory settlement of disputes.

These safeguards have not been sufficient to allay the concerns of the environmental community. Immediately upon completion, some environmental groups began a major campaign to see that CRAMRA did not come into force. Special concern was expressed about the decision not to require prior authorization for prospecting, but there was also a desire, on the part of some, to ensure that no mineral activities would ever take place. As a result of domestic pressures, the governments of France and Australia advocated a permanent ban on all mineral activity in Antarctica. U.S. environmental groups generated draft legislation calling for an indefinite ban on Antarctic mining. In 1991, the Consultative Group reached a compromise to ban Antarctic mining for 50 years and to continue the ban thereafter unless three-quarters of the consultative members vote to reverse it. These provisions are embodied in a Protocol on Environmental Protection, which by 1994 had been ratified by 10 of the 26 consultative parties, and which in effect would replace CRAMRA.

Outer Space

In outer space, the international community is facing many of the same political and management problems that it confronted in the oceans and Antarctica. The resource in question includes the use of geostationary and other orbits for activities such as telecommunications, meteorology, resource surveys, or solar power transmission. Initially a few technologically advanced countries had the capability to launch and maintain satellites. In the 1960s, the situation was one of relatively few users, and the legal regime was much like that for navigation on the high seas.

The 1967 Outer Space Treaty was agreed among the major actors in space.[4] Few developing countries took part in negotiating this treaty. The treaty adopts the laissez-faire approach of allowing free exploration and use of space, subject to the proviso that space activities be carried out for the benefit and in the interest of all countries in accordance with international law. Activities are to be pursued on the basis of equality and international cooperation in scientific research. Weapons of mass destruction are proscribed, as are military installations in space. The treaty also bans national appropriation of celestial bodies.

Although space still remains an uncrowded and underexploited area, a number of developing countries became apprehensive in the 1970s that certain space resources were, in fact, finite and that the developed countries would appropriate available resources operating under the first-come first-served principle. In particular, they were concerned about future access to geostationary orbits and the allocation of the radio spectrum.

The geostationary orbit is located 22,300 miles above the equator. At this altitude satellites can remain in a fixed position above the earth to carry out telecommunications and other activities. The minimum distance that should separate satellites in geostationary orbit to avoid interference with one another has been a function of technology. The technology of 1990 would allow about 200 geo-

4. The Treaty on Principles Governing the Activities of States in the Exploration and Use of Outer Space Including the Moon and Other Celestial Bodies.

stationary satellites to operate in the same frequency band without interfering with one another; if evenly spaced, they would be more than 800 miles apart. However, the use of directed beams and improved stabilizers, as well as other new technologies, could permit hundreds more satellites to be stationed above the equator in the relatively near future. Clearly, the possibility of allocating a thousand or more satellite positions would pose far fewer problems than the prospect of only a few hundred. Foreseeable technological advances may increase the number of available satellite slots even further.

Although there have been no internationally agreed legal definitions of where national air space ends and outer space begins, it has been widely accepted that earth orbiting satellites move in outer space. The lowest orbit for maintaining a satellite in orbit is 62 miles (apogee) to 28 miles (perigee). By this definition, the geostationary orbit would fall well beyond national air space. Despite the generally accepted norm for defining outer space, 8 equatorial nations (of 11) agreed in the 1976 Bogota Declaration to claim the geostationary orbit as part of their national territory. They argued that, since there is no explicit definition of outer space, the ban on national appropriation does not apply to them, even though their claims extend 22,300 miles above the Earth. The eight countries stated that satellites stationed over their countries must receive their prior authorization. Geostationary positions over the oceans are part of the common heritage of mankind, and, in their view, an appropriate regime should be developed. The Latin American claimants declared that they were willing to negotiate regional agreements with other Latin American parties to provide access to the geostationary locations over land.

The claims of the equatorial states have been largely ignored in practice both within the International Telecommunications Union (ITU) and the Committee on Peaceful Uses of Outer Space (COPUOS).[5] Nonetheless, they provide a striking example of the partition approach carried to an extreme.[6] They also illustrate the

5. After failing to reach satisfactory accommodation with Colombia, the United States launched a satellite above Colombia over that country's protest.
6. If pursued by all nations, it would lead to national appropriation of space amounting to nearly 75 times the volume of the earth.

anxiety of developing countries that they will be unable to exploit common property resources while technology resides in the hands of a few developed countries.[7]

Similar anxieties are apparent in the negotiations over the allocation of the radio spectrum at the meetings of the World Administrative Radio Conference (WARC), held under ITU auspices. International coordination of the use of radio frequencies has long been recognized as necessary to standardize signals and avoid interference among signals, a topic that properly belongs in chapter five.[8] In the WARC discussions, the developing countries favor reserving frequency spectra and orbital positions for themselves even though they presently have no plans to use them. The developed countries argue that this is a waste of the spectrum and of satellite positions. Instead, they point to the fact that technological progress has continued to allow an increase in the number of frequency bands available to all users. During the 1985 and 1988 WARC negotiations, a complex plan was put forward to allot each ITU nation a specific orbital location for fixed satellite services in certain newly allocated, lightly used frequency bands. "Allotment" was an assurance that a position would be available when and if the country wanted to use it, but fell short of a formal assignment of property rights to a particular location. This allotment was counterbalanced by maintenance of the traditional "as-needed" approach to assignment in the bands heavily used for commercial and military-government satellites and favored by the developed countries and the Soviet Union.

The 1992 WARC approved a U.S. proposal for a system of lower (nongeostationary) satellites for cellular communication, but with the injunction that any country putting up such a system (the U.S. firm Motorola plans to introduce a system called Iridium in the mid-1990s) must "heed" the desires of other countries to operate such systems, thus leaving potentially complex negotiations to the

7. Corrigan (1985).
8. The International Telegraphic Union was established in Paris in 1865 to coordinate telegraphic communication; the International Radiotelegraph Union was established in Berlin in 1906 to coordinate use of the newly invented radio. The two were combined in Madrid in 1932 into the International Telecommunications Union, which was reorganized as a specialized agency of the United Nations in 1947 and located in Geneva.

future. Here the main reservations were voiced by Europe and Japan, which with their denser populations prefer land-based telephone systems to a satellite system; many developing countries supported the U.S. proposal, which could potentially improve their domestic and international communications with much less investment than would be required using traditional technology.

Ocean Seabed

In addition to navigation, which remains largely laissez faire, the major exception to the partition approach in international negotiations on Law of the Sea was a collective management regime for the deep seabed. The resources of principal interest in the seabed are so-called manganese nodules (mainly nickel in terms of their value) and polymetallic sulfides. Nodules of greatest commercial value (those with the highest copper, nickel, and cobalt content) are found in the deepest part of the oceans, largely in the Pacific well beyond the limits of national jurisdiction. Early visions of vast mineral wealth led the UN General Assembly to pass a resolution in 1970 declaring the seabeds beyond national jurisdiction to be the "common heritage of mankind"—a concept that has never been defined. The most notable impact of that resolution was that many coastal states immediately laid claim to 200-mile zones and to continental margins when they extended beyond 200 miles. These claims radically accelerated trends that had been under way for decades and that were formally accepted in the draft Law of the Sea Treaty of 1982. Coastal states thereby succeeded in removing the most valuable common resources from prospective international management.

In subsequent negotiations over a regime to mine what remained of the seabed, potential mining states recommended an economically efficient approach based on a minimum of regulation. In essence, it would allow miners to explore and lay claim to seabed sites, subject to payment of royalties. Conflict with other miners would be resolved through dispute settlement among the mining states. Revenues from resource exploitation would be shared with the international community in deference to the disputed "common heritage" principle.

Developing countries interpreted the common heritage concept to mean something quite different, however. Lacking the technology and capability to mine the seabed directly, the Group of 77 proposed that a seabed mining body call the Enterprise be set up under the auspices of an International Seabed Authority (ISA), which they would control. The Enterprise would mine the seabed directly, to the exclusion of all national mining, with technology and financing provided by the developed states.

The UN Conference on Law of the Sea (UNCLOS III) treaty sought a compromise between the positions of the developed and developing countries. The compromise was based on the concept of a "parallel system," as it came to be called. On one track, private or state companies would be able to mine part of the seabed, provided they fulfilled certain conditions allowing the Enterprise to operate at the same time. These conditions began with the requirement that each company explore and submit to the ISA the coordinates for two sites of equal value. The authority would then select one for the Enterprise. Other conditions included substantial upfront financial contributions to the ISA by governments, limits on seabed production to protect competing land-based mineral producers, and mandatory transfer of technology to the Enterprise and developing countries if the mining technology is not available on the open market. In the view of the developed nations, this "compromise" imposed too many onerous and costly burdens and set unacceptable political and economic precedents. Unable to negotiate needed changes in the UN context, the United States, the Federal Republic of Germany, and the United Kingdom, among others, decided not to sign the treaty.

The developed countries subsequently worked to create a basic approach to seabed mining that addresses problems as they arise. In 1984, after resolving claims to overlapping mine sites, the United States, Britain, France, Japan, the Federal Republic of Germany, Belgium, Italy, and the Netherlands (collectively, the "reciprocating states") agreed to respect existing and future claims on the basis of who was first (in time) to make them. These claims were then published in the UN *Law of the Sea Bulletin.* In 1987, after negotiations with the Soviets to resolve conflicting claims, the Soviet and Western claims were reissued to reflect the agreed revisions.

While the reciprocating states were pursuing a pragmatic approach, the "preparatory committee" of the proposed seabed mining authority was meeting periodically to prepare for the UNCLOS treaty. Two of the reciprocating states, Japan and France, together with the USSR, which was later joined by China, India, and Korea, participated in discussions about the areas their state-sponsored mining consortia would offer as a mine site to the authority. Three private U.S. mining consortia, operating under U.S. law, declined to participate in this process.

In the intervening years, reality has intruded on the seabed mining part of UNCLOS convention, not least because the economics of seabed mining have proved to be much less attractive than was thought to be the case in the 1970s. The visible failure of centrally planned economic systems in Eastern Europe also had an impact on the UNCLOS preparatory discussions and a number of countries became willing to revisit and revise the seabed portions of the UNCLOS treaty. These negotiations matured in 1994 as an Agreement on Implementation of Part XI of the Law of the Sea Convention of 1982, which came into force formally in November 1994. They resulted in a substantial overhaul of the provisions governing the future development of seabed mining. Most of the special privileges of and the strong bias toward the Enterprise provided in the 1982 convention are eliminated by the new agreement, which applies on an interim basis until formally ratified. The Enterprise, if it is created, must operate on a sound commercial basis. In the meantime, technically qualified mining consortia can proceed to develop their approved mine sites after reserving half of each prospected area for possible joint ventures with the Enterprise.

Thus a variety of approaches to the management of ocean resources exists. The partition approach prevailed in UNCLOS III for fisheries and offshore oil. Navigation and environmental resources were left to existing international regulatory institutions with some increased obligations for coastal states. Seabed mining was addressed in an initially flawed effort at international collective management but seems to be gravitating toward partition within an internationally agreed framework of rules.

Harvesting the Oceans

Harvesting creatures from the sea is an ancient activity; it did not threaten animal populations so long as the harvesting effort was light and the technology was primitive. Increased effort and improved technologies, however, have greatly depleted a number of natural stocks, and that, in turn, has triggered international efforts to protect the stocks for future use. The first successful effort concerned the Alaskan fur seals, where a 1911 treaty among Britain (on behalf of Canada), Japan, Russia, and the United States defined harvesting conditions and limited the total harvest, mainly to preserve stocks and but also to conserve financial resources, since harvest competition was increasing at sea and since more efficient harvesting could take place on (nationally controlled) islands.[9]

The International Whaling Commission was created to monitor and limit harvesting of whales, the depletion of which was already evident in the 1920s. A total catch of 16,000 blue whale "equivalents" was allowed in the southern hemisphere, whales being reckoned by their oil relative to that of the blue whale, the world's largest animal. The first reduction in the total quota occurred in 1963 and harvesting the blue whale itself was prohibited in 1964, when fears of its extinction mounted.[10]

The United States passed the Marine Mammal Protection Act in 1972, and thereafter the United States urged a moratorium in the IWC on the harvesting of all whales. Such a moratorium was finally agreed in 1982 (over the objections of four nations, Japan, Norway, Peru, and the USSR, with Peru's objection subsequently

9. For a detailed history of the negotiations, see Natalia S. Mirovitskaya, Margaret Clark, and Ronald G. Purver, "North Pacific Fur Seals: Regime Formation as a Means of Resolving Conflict," in Young and Osherenko (1993, pp. 22–55).

10. Even after 30 years, there are reckoned to be fewer than a thousand blue whales left.

withdrawn). It came into effect in 1985 and has been subject to annual review since 1990. In 1992, Iceland announced its withdrawal from the IWC, and Norway announced its intention to resume harvesting the minke whale, a small whale deemed to have recovered substantially (to 900,000 worldwide, with an estimated 87,000 in the northeast Atlantic).[11] Both nations charged the IWC with having altered its basic objective—from assuring adequate supplies for future harvest to protecting all whales (except for small numbers allowed to be killed in the name of science). Japan also indicated a desire to resume minke whaling, but indicated that for the moment it would not ignore the consensus of other nations. In 1992, a new rule for allocating the harvest was agreed but not put into effect. The impasse continues, and whaling has resumed, with Norway allowing its whalers to take almost 300 minke whales in the 1993 season.

The difficulty here is that an action taken in the name of one widely supported objective, maintaining adequate stocks, also served another deeply felt but not-so-widely shared objective, protection of marine mammals. Several nations indicated in the early 1980s that there was no scientific basis for a (virtual) ban on harvesting all whales, only a few species. But they were carried along by the consensus for a few years. By 1992, it was abundantly clear that at least the minke was nowhere near extinction, and indeed seemed to be thriving. Then the difference between the two objectives sharpened, and international consensus disappeared. Overharvesting is not likely in the near future because the whaling communities in the three countries that want to resume whaling are small. But if they are economically successful, they may grow and, more important, they may invite new entrants from other countries, returning international whaling to the free-for-all of the 1920s.[12]

11. Betsy Carpenter and Jennifer I. Seter, "Harpoon Rattling in the Atlantic," *U.S. News & World Report*, October 18, 1993, p. 72.

12. It is noteworthy that the 1973 Agreement on Conservation of Polar Bears, the first international prohibition on hunting a land animal, came about in part because of a fear that the Japanese, who were already large purchasers of pelts, would start hunting them in the international waters of the Arctic Ocean. National protection regimes already existed, on differing terms, in the five state jurisdictions bordering the Arctic—Canada, Denmark (Greenland), Norway (Svalbard), the USSR, and the United States.

With respect to marine mammals, and Antarctica as well, issues of sensibility have become mixed with issues of conservation (that is, efficient harvesting), further complicating an already complicated international decisionmaking environment. That conflict erupted sharply over the harvesting of tuna by purse seine nets, which also led to the catch and incidental drowning of many dolphin, or more accurately porpoises. The U.S. tuna fleet was enjoined to reduce greatly its killing of porpoises, which it did at some expense. It then complained about imported tuna, whereupon the United States (on a court order) prohibited the importation of tuna caught in a manner that killed more porpoises than were allowed to the American tuna fleet, a rule that affected mainly Mexico and Venezuela, both of whose fleets operate in the eastern Pacific, where for unclear reasons porpoises and yellow-fin tuna swim close together (unlike in some other parts of the world). Mexico, a relatively new adherent to the General Agreement on Tariffs and Trade (GATT), complained that the U.S. prohibition on imports of Mexican tuna violated its GATT rights. In 1991, a GATT panel found in Mexico's favor, creating an uproar in the U.S. environmental community.

Although a detailed account of the factual circumstances and the associated legal arguments would take this book too far afield,[13] it returns to the issue below in discussing trade sanctions in pursuit of environmental objectives. The main point in this chap-

---

The original intention was to cover only international waters. But disagreements over the boundaries between national and international territory, an issue of importance in the upcoming Law of the Sea negotiations and a source of disagreement between the United States and Canada and between Norway and the USSR, led the five participants to evade the issue by agreeing on a complete prohibition on killing polar bears, subject to stipulated exceptions, even though the polar bear was far from extinction. The agreement was deliberately not made universal, on the assumption, which so far has proved correct, that if the five bordering states reached agreement, others would not challenge them. See Anne Fikkan, Gail Osherenko, and Alexander Arikainen, "Polar Bears: The Importance of Simplicity," in Young and Osherenko (1993, pp. 96–151). Thus the exigencies of international politics led to a major achievement for those interested in protecting large animals.

13. In brief, U.S. law requires banning imports of tuna from countries whose fishermen allegedly kill 1.25 times the porpoises killed by U.S. tuna fishermen, per net dropped. The U.S. Administration did not enforce this provision until compelled to do so by court order. A panel of the General Agreement on Tariffs and Trade (GATT) found the U.S. action to be inconsistent with its GATT commitments on technical grounds: (i) it violated the national treatment provision of Article III, in that it was retroactive and thus created uncertainty for

ter on global commons is that the United States took unilateral action to protect an admittedly abundant marine resource, subject to no national jurisdiction, and the method it chose (not the objective) ran afoul of an existing international agreement.

The lesson that emerges from these attempts to create international regimes for global commons is that laissez faire can be expected to work only so long as pressure on the resource is low, as in outer space and Antarctica. When that ceases to be the case, there will be a scramble for the resource, depleting it rapidly. To avoid that, the international community will face a choice between partition—the establishment of national ownership—and collective management, which can come in a variety of forms. Neither have worked especially well in the past.[14] When it comes to renewable resources, however, such as stocks of fish, some form of international collective management is likely to be more sensible than purely national management. Governments in dealing with one another will have to pay more attention to the scientific evidence on the stocks than will national governments in dealing with their own voting constituents.

The Atmosphere

In many respects our atmosphere can be viewed as a common property resource and as such raises global commons problems.

---

foreign suppliers; and (ii) it could not be justified under Article XX, which [inter alia] permits trade restrictions necessary to protect animal life, on the grounds that the action in question exceeded what was necessary, since less trade-distorting alternatives had not been exhausted and the life in question was outside the jurisdiction of the United States. In short, the panel adopted a "strict construction" interpretation of the GATT; it did not address the underlying issue of public policy. See Charnovitz (1992) and Jackson (1993) on the legal arguments against and for the position of the GATT panel. Mexico, concerned with approval of the North American Free Trade Agreement (NAFTA) by the United States, did not press for formal adoption by GATT of the panel report, so it has no formal standing. Instead, bilateral accommodation was negotiated between Mexico and the United States involving a five-year moratorium on purse seine fishing. The European Community, however, has filed a related complaint against the U.S. ban on imports of tuna from countries that import tuna from Mexico.

14. See Peterson in Haas, Keohane, and Levy (1993) on international efforts to manage fishing resources.

National activities affecting the atmosphere can have direct and indirect effects on the climate, weather, health, and resources of other countries.

A variety of ostensibly domestic or local activities may adversely affect the troposphere or the stratosphere. The conversion of forest lands to agriculture, as well as heavy reliance on fossil fuels, can increase levels of carbon dioxide production and increase the absorption of infrared radiation by the earth. Emissions, such as carbon dioxide, promote a "greenhouse effect" by trapping the sun's energy. Carried out on a massive scale, such changes raise the earth's temperature. Similarly, national policies on the use of chlorofluorocarbons (CFCs) have become a matter of international concern since the release of these chemicals reduces the capacity of the stratospheric ozone to protect creatures, including people, from the sun's ultraviolet radiation. These issues will be taken up in chapter five.

Chapter 4

Economic Activities with No Transborder Externalities

THE policy issues here are whether and under what circumstances countries should be held to similar environmental standards. If they are not, some high-polluting activities will tend to concentrate over time in those jurisdictions with laxer environmental regulations, partly through the migration of internationally mobile firms to those jurisdictions (provided other considerations do not dominate the locational decision) but mainly through the relative growth of the polluting activities in those jurisdictions and their relative decline in jurisdictions with stronger environmental regulations.[1] Exports from such locations have been pejoratively dubbed "environmental dumping."

Such an appellation is tendentious and misleading in many circumstances. In a world with many countries of diverse endowments and diverse preferences and circumstances, stiff environmental regulations—for example, with respect to air emissions—may make good sense in one setting but not in another. This is for two quite different reasons. First, the atmosphere is a natural and often effective disposal medium, so long as its disposal capacity is not overwhelmed. In some parts of the world its disposal capacity has clearly been overwhelmed, and the result is air pollution at unacceptable levels, offensive to the nose and sometimes even dangerous to the health of the population. In other parts of the world, this

1. Jaffe and others (1993) report that there is no evidence that tough U.S. environmental regulations harm the international competitiveness of U.S. firms or cause them to relocate to developing countries.

28

situation has not been and may never be reached, because of prevailing winds or the absence of a downwind population (think of the east coasts of New Zealand or southern Africa). Put another way, in some places environmental regulation may be unnecessary to achieve a favorable environmental outcome. Under these circumstances stiff antipollution requirements would impose an unnecessary social cost.

Second, in areas of dense human settlement, clear air and clean river water are goods that must compete with other goods and services in the social budget. How each community decides to allocate its limited resources will properly depend not only on the objective circumstances of the community but also on its preferences; those preferences, in turn, generally depend in part on the level of income enjoyed by the community. Clear air and clean water seem to be goods that are heavily demanded only after a certain level of material well-being, especially in terms of diet, has been achieved. In other words, rich people want proportionately more of them than poor people do.

The basic principles by which each community decides for itself how best to generate income and how best to spend it, including the mix between public and private goods, should work all right provided that the decision affects only or mainly members of the community in question. In today's world, nation-states are "communities" for these purposes. As countries develop economically, one can be reasonably confident that among other changes they will raise their standards for the local environment: first in terms of sanitation and other public health measures, including clean drinking water, then in clean ambient air and clean river and lake water.[2]

Of course, decisions on environmental matters may affect others through foreign trade, just as other policy decisions do, such as those on transportation infrastructure or educational policy. But if they adequately reflect the collective preferences and circum-

2. See World Bank (1992, p. 11). Grossman and Krueger (1993) estimate that air pollution in the form of sulfur dioxide and particulate matter rises with per capita income, peaks at around $4,000, and declines thereafter, suggesting (since industrial activity does not generally decline at higher income levels) that the public will act to reduce pollutants at higher income levels.

stances of the country, they enter into its comparative advantage in the world economy. "Dumping" from countries with lower environmental standards may therefore be a misnomer. "Full social cost" is reflected appropriately, using the valuations of the community (nation) in question. It would not be appropriate to impute the value that, say, Los Angelenos place on clean air to the citizens of Mexico City, any more than it would be appropriate to impute Tokyo real estate values to Los Angeles. *Local* valuation should be used in each case. From this perspective, it is *desirable* that production of goods that involve air or water pollution migrate from those countries where, in the view of the local community, it imposes a heavy social cost to those countries where, in the view of the local community, it does not impose a heavy social cost, for either of the two reasons given above. Thus, in the absence of transborder externalities, there is no special need for international action, beyond making clear the basic ground rules. It is a case where "mutual recognition" of national decisions is appropriate.

This conclusion will offend the sensibilities of some, and they will want to impose their standards on the residents of other countries, even in the face of charges of engaging in environmental paternalism, even environmental imperialism. Yet imposition of additional costs on the exports of developing countries, through environmental regulations, will likely lead to lower real wages in those countries, thus depressing living standards there. The export of rich countries' environmental standards thus happens at the expense of poor workers elsewhere.

Nonetheless, environmental sensitivities will sometimes become sufficiently intense and widespread that they will result in sanctions, probably involving import prohibitions, against the offending countries. As noted above, imports of tuna into the United States that have not been caught by methods that adequately protect porpoises (as defined in U.S. legislation) have been restricted. Surely the international community cannot, and should not be able to, force a country to purchase products the production of which offends the sensibilities of its citizenry.

The proper course under such circumstances is, first, to negotiate international norms to prohibit or limit the offending activity.

This starting point has the advantage that scientific evidence on any claims made with respect to the offending activity will be carefully scrutinized.

If negotiation fails, or if negotiated limits are not enforced adequately, countries may require that special labels be attached to the product, indicating that it was produced in an offensive way (such as, the catching of this tuna did not protect porpoises). Such labels may, in turn, permit consumer boycotts of the product, or at a minimum permit individuals most offended by the method of production to shun the product.[3]

Or the country may have recourse to trade sanctions, prohibiting imports of the product produced in the offensive way. But under existing trade rules, these limits against the offending country may violate trading rights that the country has acquired through previous commitments undertaken in international agreement by the sanctioning country. If rights are violated, the sanctioning country should offer compensation in other areas of trade (on the assumption comity obtains between the states in question). The sanctioning country must therefore be clear about its relative priorities.

If the compensation is deemed inadequate by the offending country, it will have the right to "retaliate" against the sanctioning country by restricting that country's exports in a magnitude that is appropriate to the trade impact of the import prohibitions.[4]

Differences in environmental standards will be seized, just as differences in labor standards have been, as an excuse for restrict-

3. The "dolphin safe" label on American-caught tuna is reported to have led to a sharp decline in tuna not so labeled, especially tuna from Mexico, even before the import ban on Mexican tuna. See Esty (1994).

4. The United States imposed import restrictions on certain products from the European Community in retaliation against the EC's prohibition of imports of hormone-fed beef from the United States and elsewhere. The United States challenged the EC to produce scientific evidence that hormone-fed beef was harmful, which the EC could not do. But European sensibilities, reflected in EC regulations, were very negative on "artificial" use of hormones, and the EC acted without scientific support. The EC tacitly accepted U.S. retaliation. Retaliation is a course to be avoided if possible, since some (unrelated) industry comes to enjoy the protection it affords. By 1992, the U.S. light-truck makers had come to think of the 25 percent U.S. tariff on light trucks as a right, even though it was introduced in the 1960s in retaliation (against the German firm Volkswagen) for the new EC policy on poultry, which limited U.S. exports of poultry to the EC.

ing imports by those who desire to lessen competition in the home market. Environmentalism may replace national security as a final refuge for protectionists. States will have to agree on ground rules to avoid abuse of legitimate concerns about the environment, and for this reason it will be sensible for governments to respond to the more intense sensibilities of their publics. But subject to these ground rules, the rule of mutual recognition provides an adequate framework for most cases.

Two qualifications to this conclusion need to be mentioned. First, local valuation of social costs presupposes that members of each community have an opportunity to register their preferences. Deep complications arise when decisions about public goods, such as clean air, are made by only a few individuals or not democratically arrived at within a given community. The former Soviet Union represents an extreme example, where despite the superior formal ability of central planning to take into account environmental externalities, compared with a market system, Soviet leaders devastated the environment in pursuit of their military and industrial objectives. It is highly likely that if Soviet citizens had more voice in the matter, less air pollution would have occurred and toxic waste would have been discarded with greater care.[5]

Formally, the current international order accepts any decisionmaking system within nations, except sometimes when a large portion of the population is actually brutalized. Over time, these arrangements may give way to greater international intrusion into domestic modes of decisionmaking, but that is a large topic beyond the scope of this book. To bear on the discussion above, it would have to be shown not only that a substantial fraction of the population had no voice in decisionmaking but also that its environmental preferences were markedly different from those reflected in the national policies. In particular, one would have to demonstrate that the authoritarian government placed less value on various aspects of the environment than the typical resident would—something that would be found in some

5. See Peterson (1993) for an account of the environmental devastation in the Soviet Union.

situations, such as the former communist countries, but not in others.[6]

One could, however, carry this line of reasoning further. Some democracies do not permit substantial numbers of foreign residents to vote (Luxembourg and Switzerland, for example); in others, many citizens choose not to vote (the United States, as compared with Europe) or their legislative bodies do not accurately reflect the composition of the public (such as the U.S. Senate). In some fledgling democracies with strong ethnic cleavages, some identifiable groups are regularly out-voted, and even exploited, by the dominant majority.[7] Such societies tend to be politically unstable, indulging in coups and civil wars, leading eventually to authoritarian rule. But the authoritarian rulers may have more sensitivity to the views of minorities than did rule by a majority ethnic group.

Furthermore, it is not clear that this concern about collective community decisions should be limited to environmental issues. It is well known that different democracies take different views with respect to the distribution of income, with Scandinavians being considerably more egalitarian than Anglo-Saxons, and that the distribution of income can influence national factor and commodity prices. Should differences in social legislation, such as minimum wages or national health care or severance pay, be actionable on the grounds that countries with less egalitarian systems are engaged in "social dumping," as some French officials recently suggested with respect to Britain?

There is need for greater external pressure on nondemocratic governments, especially when it is suspected the rulers are paying less attention to environmental issues than the typical resident would like, or when strong minority interests are being systematically overridden. But the pressure should be aimed at improving the civil and political rights of the residents, rather than at specific policy outcomes preferred by foreigners. When relatively rich Americans and Europeans attempt to impose their environmental views

6. Some tropical deforestation, for instance, has been done by local Brazilians for crop growing or cattle grazing despite efforts by the central government to limit cutting. See "Disappearing Jungles: The Culprits," *The Economist*, September 4, 1993, p. 86.

7. Horowitz (1994).

on other countries, in matters in which they do not have a direct interest, they can properly be charged with eco-imperialism.

The second possible qualification to the proposition that no international action is required on local environmental externalities concerns instances in which countries share objectives but do not act because of short-run costs to exports, output, and employment.

Suppose each of several countries has a preference function that includes, say, steel production and clean air. If production is mobile, each country will be inhibited from introducing clean air requirements by fear of losing steel production (and jobs) to countries that have less stringent pollution requirements. Since, by assumption, the countries have similar preferences, there is a case here for collective action: if all improve their air requirements together, production will have no incentive to move (on grounds of pollution regulations) and the countries will have cleaner air.

This kind of example is surely what many people have in mind when they urge common standards for pollution across countries. A critical assumption in the example, however, is that each community desires to have *steel* production. But suppose our objective is not steel production per se, but higher standards of living. If producing steel is a polluting activity, but steel is desirable, communities that are less sensitive to the emissions (for whatever reason) should, all other things equal, produce steel for all. Other communities should produce other products and trade them for steel. All can potentially be made better off in terms of their own preferences and circumstances. Each country should act to reduce unwanted pollution on its own; if two or more communities have similar preferences and circumstances, they will both act, minimizing the movement of steel production between them.

The objections to this impeccable economic line of reasoning are political, apart from those that arise from misunderstanding. They assume, first, that, if steel production is lost, employment and incomes will decline—a failure of balance of payments adjustment and macroeconomic management. Or they assume that, even if total employment is maintained, steel workers will still be losers because they will find less attractive jobs or none at all—a failure to distribute well the benefits of the relocation (this is, of course, a potential problem with *all* dislocating change). Both of these arguments may have some validity in the short run but are invalid in the long run (when all existing steel workers would have retired even if production did not relocate) that is presumably relevant for durable environmental improvement.[8]

So long as economies remain flexible and near full employment (an important macroeconomic condition for smooth microeconomic adjustment), they should have little trouble adjusting to changing standards, environmental or otherwise, provided major changes are introduced over a sensible period of time. There is no long-run competition between employment and environmental conditions imposed on production. It is true, however, that rapid cost-increasing changes that fall disproportionately across industries in an environment of vigorous international competition might well result in plant closings that would not occur either in an environment protected from import competition or one in which the required changes are introduced more gradually.[9] So tension will exist between those who want to improve environmental conditions rapidly and those who want to maintain a competitive economic system with foreign competition playing an important role.

---

8. Environmentalists, however, may be playing the domestic political game correctly. Business interests are usually politically influential, and they provide "jobs," an important political currency. The threat of particular jobs lost to foreign locations may therefore inhibit environmental action. An international agreement holding other countries to similar standards helps to neutralize this argument (as Mexico's President Carlos Salinas attempted to in the debate over NAFTA by pointing to stiff environmental standards for all new investment in Mexico). Environmentalists may therefore favor such agreements even if they have no direct interest in environmental conditions in the other countries.

9. The short-run macroeconomics of rapidly introduced cost-increasing environmental regulations on production in internationally competitive industries are complicated. The stiffer regulations (or taxes) will induce some job losses in the most affected activities because of international competition. On the other hand, in the absence of that competition, domestic prices will rise more rapidly, and in pursuit of price stability the monetary authorities will tighten credit conditions, thus leading to a loss of aggregate employment in the short run. Although it would perhaps be more concentrated on particular industries, the first effect would not necessarily be larger than the second, so it is not clear that even in the short run employment would be hurt more because of international competition. International coordination of actions might help a bit, but not much if other countries are also all concerned about "inflation." All rapid changes introduce dislocations.

These concerns do not seem to have had a major influence on environmental decisionmaking in the major industrial countries; rather, Japan, the United States, and European countries were driven to action in the 1960s and 1970s mainly by increasingly unacceptable local environmental conditions. The fact that similar movements developed in all these regions, even without formal coordination, may have encouraged them to be more aggressive than they otherwise would have been; and perhaps they would have been even more aggressive had they coordinated their actions more closely. But where local externalities are concerned the policy choices are *not* generally characterized by a Prisoner's Dilemma, whereby both of two (or more) parties are better off if they cooperate, but each is worse off if it acts alone. Communities should and generally do reflect their own collective preferences; transitional problems can be handled when long-term objectives are being pursued. Trade liberalization typically involves phase-in periods of 5 to 15 years; the same can be true for environmental regulations or taxes.

Competition among newly industrializing countries for export markets may slow down the pace at which they adopt stiffer environmental regulations as their incomes rise and their local environments deteriorate. Thus, some practical advantage may flow when similarly situated developing countries coordinate both the timing and the content of their environmental regulations. But they should not hold back from pursuing desired improvements if such coordination cannot be arranged.

Chapter 5

Economic Activities with Transborder Externalities

*I*N situations where the actions in one country have an environmental impact in other countries, or in international domains which other countries use, the appropriate policy response depends upon the distinction between *local* transborder externalities and *global* externalities. Most externalities, such as effluent into a river that traverses two or more countries, or air pollution that drifts across national boundaries, are regional. They call for international action, but not for global action. Handling the waters of the Colorado or the Rio Grande is a matter for Mexico and the United States, the Nile for Egypt and the Sudan. Acid rain, so far as is known, is largely regional in its impacts.[1]

This fact is acknowledged in practice, and there are numerous examples of regional monitoring or management pacts involving two or more nations. For example, a number of European countries agreed in 1985 to reduce their sulfur emissions by 30 percent and in 1988 to freeze their emissions of nitrogen oxides, both thought to be important contributors to acid rain, which does not respect national boundaries.[2] Attempts by bordering countries to limit both land- and sea-based pollution of the North and Baltic

1. Some acid rain may have global effects. The origins of arctic haze in northern Alaska have been traced to Europe, several thousand miles away. U.S.-Mexican cooperation on water rights and disposition of sewage have a history going back nearly a century. See Weintraub (1990) and Hufbauer and Schott (1992).

2. European nonsignatories have reduced their sulfur emissions since 1985, but signatories have reduced theirs even more. The reductions have often greatly exceeded 30 percent, however, suggesting that strong domestic pressures in each country were the

Seas, which was damaging fisheries of importance to those countries, date back to the early 1970s, as do less successful attempts to control pollution in the Mediterranean.[3] Attempts to manage fisheries on a regional basis have an even older history.[4] Japan has financed several stack scrubbers in China to reduce sulfur emissions from use of high-sulfur coal, since the pollution moves eastward to Japan.[5]

In contrast to these many regional issues, only a few issues command actual or potential interest around the globe. Atmospheric testing of nuclear weapons provides an early example, as it became evident that radioactive fallout was widely spread around the world. A more recent example is provided by the depletion of the stratospheric ozone layer, which protects the earth's surface from ultraviolet radiation. Less well known is the use of the electromagnetic spectrum for short-wave radio and other transmissions, where without some allocative system broadcasts would interfere with one another's reception. Potentially most dramatic is global climate change resulting from greenhouse gas emissions or other anthropogenic activity. Because of high stratospheric winds, certain emissions get transported great distances and thoroughly mixed. They potentially affect everyone.

This chapter will provide a detailed analysis of global climate change as an issue calling for international attention. The chapter begins with a discussion of the new international regime for ozone, which matured earlier than concern over global climate change. As

---

dominant factor, not the international agreement. Haas (Peter M. Haas, "Protecting the Baltic and North Seas," in Haas, Keohane, and Levy, 1993) argues that the agreement was influential in getting countries to reexamine their own interests, partly by encouraging research and disseminating information about the effects of acid rain of which some governments were not aware, partly by providing a forum for active countries to put pressure on the laggard countries, and partly by providing authoritative information to private groups that were pressing for reduced emissions.

3. For details on the North and Baltic Seas, see Marc A. Levy, "European Acid Rain: The Power of Tote-Board Diplomacy," in Haas, Keohane, and Levy (1993, pp. 75–132). For the Mediterranean, see Baruch Boxer, "The Mediterranean Sea: Preparing and Implementing a Regional Action Plan," in Kay and Jacobson (1983, pp. 267–309).

4. M. J. Peterson, "International Fisheries Management," in Haas, Keohane, and Levy (1993, pp. 249–305).

5. Stone (1993) provides additional examples.

such, the history of efforts to reduce ozone offers some insights into the future of cooperation on global climate change.

Ozone Depletion

Stratospheric ozone, a molecule of oxygen formed by three atoms instead of the normal two, filters out ultraviolet radiation from the sun, thus protecting creatures on the surface of the earth from surface damage (to eyes and skin) and possible genetic change. Its possible destruction by a useful, and previously thought harmless, class of man-made chemicals, chlorofluorocarbons, widely used for refrigerants, insulation, cleaning solvents, and in aerosols, was first conjectured in 1974. The first National Academy of Sciences (NAS) analysis of the impact of CFCs on the ozone layer was not initially accepted by the European scientific and policy communities, although it was taken seriously in the United States, where it led in 1978 to the prohibition of CFCs in aerosols. Early U.S. and Nordic efforts to introduce international control of the use of CFCs failed, largely because of the unwillingness of most European governments to acknowledge a connection between CFCs and ozone depletion. In the early Reagan administration, the U.S. government also adopted the position that not enough was known to act further on CFC emissions, since such actions would be costly to users. At about the same time, the European scientific community became more concerned with ozone depletion and Nordic governments took the lead in pressing for measures to reduce CFC emissions.

Then a startling and alarming confirmation of the theoretical occurred: in 1984, scientists discovered a large and unexpected "hole" in the stratospheric ozone layer over Antarctica. While it could not be traced with certainty to CFCs (although that was definitively confirmed by late 1987), it provided strong circumstantial evidence that the emission of CFCs was causing a dangerous global effect. That finding galvanized governments into action, and in September 1987 they agreed in the Montreal Protocol (to a 1985 Vienna framework convention) on halving by the year 2000 the production and consumption of CFCs in the industrialized countries, from their levels in 1986.[6] Special, but transitional, arrangements were made for developing countries at their insistence. Further work on substitute products along with continuing scientific concern about the persistence of chlorine compounds in the upper atmosphere led the governments of the industrialized countries in 1990 to amend the Montreal Protocol by calling for the elimination of the production and consumption of CFCs by 2000.[7]

Agreement on the phasing out of CFCs was made possible by the convergence of several important factors, not likely to be present in other circumstances. First, adequate substitutes for CFCs seemed available at reasonable cost (research on substitutes had been stimulated by the early concern about CFC aerosols), although this assumption has not proved correct for some of their uses. Second, relatively few firms in relatively few countries produced CFCs, so establishing and monitoring limitations would be relatively easy. Third, one or more countries took a strong lead in pushing the negotiations forward. Fourth, and not least, a scientific hypothesis was given strong empirical support by the unexpected appearance of the ozone hole over Antarctica, which helped clinch the Montreal agreement on reductions in CFC production; empirical evidence also converged strongly toward the hypothesis by 1990, when the London phase-out was agreed.[8]

Developing countries extracted agreement from the developed countries that they could take ten years longer to phase out CFC consumption and that the developed countries would bear some of the cost of their doing so. An interim fund of $240 million, covering three years, was established to help developing countries in their phase-out (conditional on China and India signing the protocol, which both have indicated they would do). The devel-

6. The agreed 50 percent cut was a compromise between a preferred 95 percent cut by the United States and the Nordic countries and a freeze at 1986 levels favored by the European Community.

7. See Benedick (1991) and Edward A. Parson, "Protecting the Ozone Layer," in Haas, Keohane, and Levy (1993, pp. 27–73).

8. See Benedick (1991); Alice Enders and Amelia Porges, "Successful Conventions and Conventional Success: Saving the Ozone Layer," in Anderson and Blackhurst (1992, pp. 130–44); and Parson in Haas, Keohane, and Levy (1993).

oped countries also agreed to make relevant technology available "on fair and most favorable" terms. The protocol also included some provisions for restricting trade in CFCs with nonsignatories, an issue that is taken up below.

Global Climate Change

Carbon dioxide and water vapor, the principal products of normal combustion, along with ozone, CFCs, methane, and some nitrogen oxides have the attribute of being transparent to the sun's radiation but partially opaque to the earth's attempt to re-radiate the energy it receives from the sun. With the accumulation (mainly) of carbon dioxide and water vapor in the atmosphere over the aeons, this "greenhouse effect" has made life possible on earth, by warming its surface by about 30°C.

Since the beginning of the industrial revolution, carbon dioxide concentrations in the atmosphere have risen by more than 25 percent, from 275 parts per million to 350 parts per million, and further economic development based on hydrocarbon fuels holds the prospect of similar increases in the future.[9] This incontrovertible trend has given rise to concern about a gradual warming of the earth's surface and with it unpredictable changes in climate that may affect agricultural output and other living conditions, as well as raise sea levels (partly because of melting glaciers but mainly because of the thermal expansion of the oceans) that will inundate low-lying areas of settlement. On current trends, a doubling of atmospheric carbon dioxide can be expected by the middle of the twenty-first century, and the current (but disputed) consensus is that would be associated with an increase in the *equilibrium* average

9. See National Academy of Sciences (1991). The "radiative forcing" of greenhouse gases—their tendency to raise atmospheric temperature—is complicated: on a per-molecule basis, CFCs are several thousand times more potent than carbon dioxide (CO_2), and methane (CH_4) is at least ten times more potent. But methane has a much shorter life in the atmosphere than CO_2, being broken down by chemical reactions in a decade or so; and CO_2 emissions are much more abundant, so most analyses focus on CO_2. By one estimate, CO_2 accounts for about two-thirds of the anthropogenic radiative forcing. Water vapor is an important greenhouse gas, but atmospheric concentrations are maintained in equilibrium with the oceans, so human sources affect the atmosphere's water vapor only indirectly—by raising atmospheric temperature through other means, thus increasing evaporation.

surface temperature of the earth of about 2.5°C, a rise in the observed average temperature of 2.3°C by the year 2100 (owing to lags in response), and a rise in sea level of 66 centimeters (26 inches) by 2100.[10] As will be discussed below, great uncertainty surrounds these estimates.

The international community responded to these possible developments, which remain conjectural since there is little evidence of the predicted warming over the past century, by adopting at the UN Conference on the Environment and Development (UNCED) in June 1992 at Rio de Janeiro, Brazil, a Framework Convention on Climate Change. The convention states as its ultimate objective the stabilization of greenhouse gas concentrations in the atmosphere at a level that would prevent dangerous anthropogenic interference with the climate system (article 2). In pursuit of this objective, the convention calls on all signatories to facilitate research, provide information, and generally to take climate change considerations into account when framing their social, economic, and environmental policies. In addition, the developed countries (defined as the members of the Organization for Economic Cooperation and Development (OECD), the eastern European countries, except Albania, and the European countries to emerge from the former Soviet Union, including Russia) undertake to adopt national policies to limit greenhouse gas emissions (other than the CFCs already covered by the Montreal Protocol on ozone), with the aim of returning "individually or jointly" to emission levels of 1990 (article 4.2).[11] Deadlines were imposed for the submission of plans but not for the attainment of objectives. Countries such as Greece, Portugal, and Spain were unsure they could meet the objective individually, but they are allowed some room for expansion insofar as other members of the European Community make up the difference. East European countries are known to use coal and oil, the main sources of carbon dioxide emissions, inefficiently, and thus could expect to meet the objective through more efficient

10. Cline (1992, p. 107).

11. In this respect, the Rio Convention goes beyond the Vienna Convention of 1985 on ozone depletion, which focused on identifying the problem and defining objectives for monitoring developments. The policy commitments came two years later in the Montreal Protocol.

use of energy and changes in industrial structure away from heavy industry. Turkey, an OECD member with neither of these possibilities, declined to sign the convention; South Korea and Taiwan indicated that they would respect the objectives.

Developing country signatories accept the general concern and ultimate objective expressed by the convention, and they agree to cooperate toward that end, but only insofar as the OECD countries (including the European Community) finance the full incremental costs of their participation (article 4.3), which in the first instance mainly concerns collecting and providing information, along with facilitating research. All signatories accept that "economic and social development and poverty eradication are the first and overriding priorities of the developing country Parties" (article 4.7).[12] In short, to the extent that mitigating actions are to be undertaken in the relatively near future, they will have to be financed by the rich countries of the world.

Today's rich countries were responsible for most of the anthropogenically generated greenhouse gases, although tropical deforestation, rice growing, and cattle also make important contributions. The developed countries as defined in the 1992 Rio convention accounted for about 70 percent of carbon dioxide emissions, other than from deforestation, with developing countries as a group accounting for the rest.[13] But according to various "business-as-usual" scenarios involving growth in energy consumption, the 29 percent share of developing countries rises to amounts ranging from 49 to 57 percent by the year 2100, or over half of the anthropogenic carbon emissions.[14] Obviously, if developed countries cut back their emissions, as they agreed in the Rio Convention, and developing countries fail to do so, this rise in the developing country share will be even greater. Stabilization of atmospheric concentrations of greenhouse gases, as called for by the convention, will sooner or later require participation by the developing countries.

12. As printed in International Energy Agency (1992, p. 164).

13. Allowance for methane—from cattle and rice production—and for deforestation would increase the 1990 contribution of developing countries to greenhouse gas emissions.

14. Cline (1992, p. 337).

China is of special concern. It already provides 11 percent of the world's CO_2 emissions, tied for second place with Russia.[15] China's energy consumption is growing rapidly, related to its rapid economic growth in recent years, and China depends on coal for energy more than most countries, since it owns coal in abundance. Because of its higher carbon content, coal emits more carbon dioxide per unit of available energy than other fossil fuels do. And the emissions are especially great if coal is used inefficiently, as it is in China (as well as in Russia, Poland, and Ukraine).[16] At recent rates of growth, admittedly unlikely to be continued for long, and without more efficient energy use, China's share of carbon dioxide output could be expected to grow to 43 percent of the world total by 2020. As other developing countries grow, they too, can be expected to increase their energy consumption.[17]

How seriously should the problem of greenhouse warming be taken in terms of framing economic and other policies in the near future? Its perceived importance will shape the willingness of developing countries to cooperate in the reduction of greenhouse gas emissions, and it will influence the willingness of the rich countries to transfer funds to developing countries for that and related purposes. In this connection, it should be noted that a reduction of emissions to the 1990 level by the year 2000, a target widely espoused and formally adopted by several European governments and notionally by the European Community, is difficult to rationalize, other than as a device to focus the attention of policymakers and the public on the issue. In 1990, the world was emitting six to seven billion tons of carbon, and carbon dioxide concentrations in the atmosphere were rising.[18] At that level of emissions, concentrations may be expected to

15. International Energy Agency (1992, p. 130).
16. Total primary energy per dollar of 1985 GDP was about four times higher in China than in the average OECD country in 1990; in Poland, it was 3.6 times higher. The same figure for India, Mexico, and South Korea is about 60 percent higher than the OECD country average. International Energy Agency (1992, pp. 28–29).
17. In a plausible projection used in the OECD's general equilibrium environmental model (GREEN), China's share of energy-related carbon emissions grows from 11 percent of the world total in 1990 to 29 percent in 2050; India's share grows from 2.5 percent to almost 8 percent; and the OECD share falls from 47 percent to 25 percent, lower than China's. Oliveira-Martins and others (1992, p. 11).
18. Cline (1992).

continue to rise. It is atmospheric concentration, not emission, that causes the warming.

Florentin Krause, Wilfred Bach, and Jonathan Koomey have addressed this issue in an austere way. Their basic argument is as follows. The influence of greenhouse gases on the earth's surface temperature is incontrovertible. Man has been emitting these gases in large and increasing volumes for the past century and more. There is much uncertainty concerning the quantitative impact of anthropogenic emissions, but the stakes in global climate change are so high that our planning should be based on the worst plausible case, not best estimates. Historic temperature records suggest that since the advent of man two million years ago the earth has not been more than 2.0–2.5°C warmer than it is now, so this should mark the prudent upper limit on future warming.[19]

Such a maximum, combined with worst plausible case interpretations of the scientific uncertainty (including those concerning the transitory period from emission to ultimate temperature change), implies that man can emit only an additional 300 billion tons of fossil carbon—on the assumptions that production of CFCs is reduced to zero by 2000, as required by the London amendment to the Montreal protocol; that emissions of methane and N_2O are reduced; and that nonfossil carbon storage is returned to mid-1980s levels through a program of reforestation. This total allotment compares with annual emissions of nearly six billion tons of carbon today. Many time trajectories are possible within a given allowable increase in stock; postponement implies more rapid declines later. Krause, Bach, and Koomey urge that annual fossil carbon emissions should be reduced by 80 percent over the next 80 years. This worst-case scenario reflects a high degree of aversion to environmental risk, a topic to be taken up below, and leaves an economist (and should leave a policymaker) extremely uncomfortable, since it presumes benefits without attempting to calculate them and is unconcerned with the costs of achieving the desired outcome.

What provides a more appropriate basis for public policy? Society takes for granted the objective of leaving a desirable world to

19. Krause, Bach, and Koomey (1992, p. 27).

our children and our great grandchildren. One cannot anticipate their preferences, but one can try to ensure that they have at least as many opportunities and options as earlier generations have had. With that in mind, policy actions, including those with respect to climate change, should be seen as investments and therefore should be compared with alternative investments as vehicles for bequeathing a desirable world. These alternative investments include the conventional ones of an enlarged physical capital stock, including infrastructure, but also the intangible ones of education and advancing the frontiers of knowledge.[20]

Actions to mitigate excessive greenhouse warming that are costless should clearly be undertaken, since by assumption they do not compete with alternative investments. But most actions have some cost, and some of the actions proposed, such as a drastic reduction in the consumption of fossil fuels over a relatively short period of time, entail substantial costs in terms of dislocation and forgone income. Incurring those costs will be worthwhile only if they are ultimately recovered in terms of improved welfare—in the case at hand, avoidance of disastrous changes in climate—and only if the gain is greater than that on alternative investments.

The strategic alternatives are posed schematically in figure 1. There the horizontal axis measures the passage of time, and the vertical axis measures real income, net of the costs required to generate it. On the basis of past experience and current knowledge, one can assume that real income will continue to grow as technology advances and capital is accumulated, as shown in schedule 1. The prospect of greenhouse warming, however, suggests that simple extrapolation of past practices is not possible, since climate change will reduce real income in a variety of ways, such as in schedule 2, which as drawn still shows some increase in incomes over time. The most dire predictions point to a decline in incomes, which would lead to a downward-sloping schedule 2 after some point. If schedule 1 is not possible, however, neither is schedule 2

---

20. Societies late in the next century can be left to safeguard the century after that, since if our generation performs adequately they will have both better knowledge and more options for dealing with the problems they and their grandchildren will face, just as we have both better knowledge and more options than those who lived a century ago. This proposition presumes that actions today do not presage avoidable catastrophe a century hence.

Figure 1. *Greenhouse Warming: Strategic Alternatives*
Real income

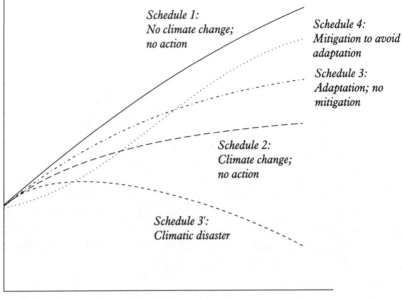

Time

likely, since as climate change becomes evident, societies will take adaptive actions—building sea walls, constructing dams for irrigation of desiccated areas, developing new seeds appropriate to the new climate, and so on. Because those actions will be costly, they produce schedule 3, which lies below schedule 1. It will, however, lie above schedule 2, since adaptive actions that do not improve schedule 2 will not knowingly be undertaken. Actions taken in the near future to mitigate climate change so as to avoid serious consequences in the more distant future are indicated in schedule 4, which is depicted below schedules 1, 2, and 3 in the near future (reflecting costly actions now that reduce income available for consumption or other investments) but above schedules 2 and 3 in the more distant future, since large-scale climate change will have been avoided.

The relevant comparison is between schedule 3, adaptation to climate change as it occurs, something societies will surely do, and schedule 4, actions taken now to avoid climate change in the future (mitigation, for short). Mixed strategies are certainly possible, since many actions are encompassed by each of these broad categories. But for purposes of analysis it is useful to keep them distinct.

The investment nature of the issue is clear: compared with adaptation, mitigation involves lower income in the near future and higher income in the more distant future. The appropriate course of action therefore depends on how one values the future with respect to the present: it depends on the choice of a discount rate to be applied to future as opposed to present income. A high discount rate will give relatively greater weight to the near-term costs of mitigation and less weight to the more distant costs of adaptation than would a low discount rate.

One further observation should be made. Since policy decisions are made by nation-states, a cost-benefit comparison such as that reflected in figure 1 must be made at the national level. The results may differ from country to country, partly because schedules 3 and 4 will bear different relationships to one another and partly because in the absence of a perfect world capital market nations will appropriately apply different discount rates when comparing the two schedules. Some countries may find mitigating action attractive while others do not. Indeed, it is even theoretically possible that *no* country would find mitigation attractive, in the sense that the present discounted value of future income under mitigation falls short of the present discounted value of future income under adaptation, yet mitigating actions should be undertaken in that the present discounted value of future world income under mitigation would exceed the corresponding value under adaptation. This paradoxical outcome would arise if those nations expecting to experience large gains from mitigation also faced substantial costs to mitigation, while countries with small gains from mitigation faced low costs to mitigation. Since greenhouse gas-induced climate change has a global source, with little-known relevance to the geographic source of the greenhouse gases, global income would be enhanced under these circumstances if the high mitigation-cost countries financed mitigating actions in the low mitigation-cost countries to the mutual benefit of both.

An *efficient* global solution involves comparing the (discounted) incremental cost of mitigation anywhere in the world with the (discounted) costs of adaptation anywhere in the world and arranging if necessary for a payment from the expected beneficiary to those who bear the cost. (Figure 1 therefore represents global schedules.)

William Cline provides a detailed application of the type of global cost-benefit analysis framed in figure 1.[21] He takes an horizon of about 300 years and presents a bold and unique attempt to calculate in some detail the economic costs associated with the warming that would take place over this period. Cline argues that the estimates associated with the scientific consensus, combined with his projections of "business as usual," lead to an average warming of 10°C over this period, beyond which little further warming is likely to take place because of heat absorption into the deep oceans. This degree of warming, assuming it were not associated with several possible but unlikely catastrophes, would lead to a gradual rise in economic costs, reaching about 6 percent of global gross domestic product in 2275.

Cline combines the estimates of several other analysts on the costs of mitigating greenhouse gas emissions and suggests that after a transition period they should be reduced to 4 billion tons of carbon a year, compared with 6 to 7 billion tons in 1990 and 82 percent below the assumed baseline projection of carbon emissions (22 billion tons) in 2100. On Cline's synthetic calculation, this cost would rise quickly to a peak of almost 4 percent of world GDP in 2040 and decline gradually to an assumed 2½ percent thereafter. The cost curve crosses the benefit curve (the latter being the costs of avoided warming) in around 2155.[22]

At a discount rate of 2 percent, which Cline argues is appropriate, the costs of warming do not justify the costs of the abatement program urged by Cline based on the central projections. But allowance for aversion to the possibility of much more serious warming than in these central projections could tilt the calculation the other way, making expenditures on mitigation worthwhile.

21. Cline (1992, pp. 130–3, chap. 7).
22. Cline (1992, pp. 277, 280).

Cline himself urges an active two-phase program of mitigation, starting with the known low-cost measures to reduce greenhouse gas emissions (or provide carbon sinks, as in reforestation) and a strong program of research, and proceeding to more costly mitigation measures in the second phase if the research suggests the desirability of proceeding.

William Nordhaus has also attempted a global cost-benefit analysis of greenhouse warming in a global optimizing model (with no distinctions made among regions).[23] By his calculations, the optimal (economically justified) degree of mitigation involves cutbacks of about 15 percent by 2100 from baseline projections, modest compared with Cline's proposal of an 80 percent reduction. The optimal trajectory would require a carbon tax of about $5 a ton in the next decade, rising to $20 a ton by the end of the next century. Nordhaus also undertakes some calculations that allow explicitly for uncertainty.

Cline's analysis, notable for its honesty and full disclosure, suffers from a stretch to assign costs to a warmer climate. Some cost calculations are imaginative but doubtful, such as computing a minimum value that Americans place on biodiversity based on the willingness to give up annual timber income of $160 million for the sake of the spotted owl (generalized to the U.S. valuation of the loss of *all* world species at $4 billion on a doubling of atmospheric carbon dioxide), despite the fact that the debate surrounding the spotted owl has manifestly used the issue of an endangered species as a narrow legal handle on the much broader question of the rate at which forests that are over 300 years old and ecologically magnificent should be depleted, even without the prospect of species loss.[24]

Some of the cost calculations are done by taking a one-sided look at the possibilities, such as the assumption that hurricane damage will rise.[25] Some impute costs to adjustment where none

23. Nordhaus (1994).

24. Cline (1992, p. 106).

25. Warming, by general agreement, will occur more at high latitudes than in the tropics, thus reducing the geographic temperature gradient and on that account reducing the prospect for large storms. On the other hand, some have suggested that temperatures at high altitudes will rise less than at the earth's surface, and the increase in vertical tempera-

should exist, such as Cline's estimate that $1.7 billion for leisure activities as ski areas must move north. Where change is slow, perceptible, and anticipated, as it would be with global warming, replacement investment must in any case take place for almost all human activities, and this replacement investment can often adapt to modestly different circumstances, including changes in location, at no incremental social cost.[26]

Second, Cline develops a careful but ultimately unpersuasive argument that future costs and benefits should be discounted at 2 percent a year in real terms. Here is not the place to go into the complicated question of discounting.[27] The central objection to 2 percent is that the world today has numerous opportunities to invest at much higher rates of return, and we do a *disservice* to future generations if we give up better investment opportunities. Cline's argument for 2 percent hinges on funds for mitigation being taken from consumption rather than from investment, via a fuel tax. But the opportunity cost of such actions remains the high-yield investments that are forgone: if one can raise funds cheaply, one still should apply them, for the sake of future generations, to high-yield investments, including education, which in developing countries is estimated to yield well more than 10 percent, and as much as 27 percent in the case of primary education in some Asian countries.[28] A review of more than a thousand World

---

ture gradient, if it occurs in tropical latitudes, may increase the likelihood and severity of hurricanes. The science panel of the Intergovernmental Panel on Climate Change took an agnostic position on storms, but Cline (1992, p. 131) opts for the possibility of increased damage to the United States at 1990 costs of $0.8 billion on a doubling of atmospheric CO_2.

26. The passage of time automatically releases both labor and capital resources from all economic activities. Often new resources are deployed in the ongoing activity, but they need not be. That the sons of coal miners have often not become coal miners does not represent a social cost; that gross earnings (including depreciation) from some activities are not reinvested in those activities also does not represent a social loss. Nordhaus (1994) simply assumes that the damage to the world economy from rising temperatures, relative to gross world product, is a function of the square of the rise in temperature multiplied by a constant calculated by aggregating from a number of sectoral studies.

27. See Nordhaus (1994, chapter 6) for an excellent discussion. Nordhaus's main calculations use a discount rate of 6 percent in the near future, falling gradually toward 3 percent near the end of the twenty-first century. Note that a positive discount rate, based on opportunity cost, is not at all inconsistent with a pure rate of time preference of zero, which treats future generations on a par with the present generation.

28. Psacharopoulos (1985, p. 586).

Bank projects suggests a prospective average rate of return of 16 percent at completion, and even in the United States investments yield over 10 percent.[29] To justify investments expected to yield only 2 percent over the next century or more would require that yields on alternative investments fall below 2 percent in the future *and* that investments in greenhouse mitigation must take place in the near future to yield as much as 2 percent. There is no basis for making either of these assumptions.

Both of these factors tilt Cline's analysis toward mitigation, but even with these biases cost-benefit calculation does not support mitigation. Cline also exaggerates the costs of adaptation to climate change, but by the same token he also probably exaggerates the costs of mitigation, in both cases because cost-reducing technical change in the future will be prompted by circumstances that are hard to predict in detail now.[30]

Cline's analysis, along with most others, necessarily centers on a mainline or central case. But the dominant characteristic of prospects for climate change and its social impacts is how *little* is actually known. Much interesting work has been done, and consensus is emerging on some issues, but in general ignorance of the topic is vast. Much uncertainty surrounds the scientific dimensions of climate change (including the all-important regional effects around the globe), the social and economic impacts of given changes in climate, and the costs of adaptation to such changes. For the last, the rate of change is usually more important than the future level, and little is known about the rate at which the climate will change. The fact that change is likely to be slow greatly reduces the costs of adapting to it, for the reasons noted above. Flexibility, however, may be low in some hard-hit poor countries, with the

29. Pöhl and Mihaljek (1989).

30. Cline (1992) allows for cost-reducing technical change in mitigation costs but arbitrarily sets these costs at a minimum of 2.5 percent of GDP in more distant years, thus denying technological change from reducing costs further, which they would almost certainly do.

Drawing on his own and other work, Nordhaus (1994) assumes that mitigation costs, relative to gross world product (GWP), are a function of (almost) the cube of the percentage reduction in greenhouse gas emissions below the baseline trajectory, with no explicit allowance for future technical change. His formulation involves very low costs for modest reductions. For instance, a 10 percent reduction from baseline would cost 0.009 percent of GWP; a 50 percent reduction, on the other hand, would cost nearly 1 percent of GWP.

possibility of engendering regional conflict and mass migration. That offers at least one reason for fostering economic development, with its improved capacity to adapt. That, in turn, provides some support to the developing countries that at the Rio conference emphasized development rather than environment. It also provides reason in a world of scarce public funds for developed countries to worry about investments in low-yield mitigation actions if it involves giving up high-yield investments that foster economic development.

Risk Aversion

It is widely taken for granted that people dislike uncertainty; they have an aversion to risk and are willing to pay to reduce it. This attitude underlies the willingness of individuals to take out fire and liability insurance: to pay a known cost (the insurance premium) to mitigate the possibly high costs of uncertain and perhaps even improbable events.

Given current information, the uncertainties associated with mitigating global climate change and its attendant costs are at least as great—probably greater—than the uncertainties associated with other forms of investment. On that account, it will perhaps be concluded that costly mitigation actions should not be undertaken. However, the payoff from mitigation actions today will be greatest if global climate change and the associated costs turn out to be large. Of course, if the costs associated with global climate change are low, any investment in mitigation will have a low or negligible return. But such investment may still be worthwhile as insurance against an uncertain but possibly costly contingency.

How do these considerations influence the discount rate? The precise answer is not straightforward, unless the uncertainty itself is related in a particular way to the passage of time. Roughly speaking, however, one can say that where an uncertain outcome (the future payoff from mitigation) is negatively correlated with overall economic prospects, and where the uncertainty grows exponentially with time, some deduction from the discount rate used to evaluate mitigation is warranted. How much depends on the nature of the uncertainty, an issue that needs greater discussion, and on the degree of society's risk aversion. But presumably it was this sort of consideration that led U.S. policymakers in 1980 to stipulate a discount rate of only 7 percent for publicly financed energy-related projects, 3 percentage points lower than the general standard for government investments. Serious disturbances in the energy sector, unlike other sectors, can lower gross national product significantly, so some component of the energy investment can be regarded as an insurance premium whose purpose is to mitigate the economic impact of large disturbances in the world oil market.

Nordhaus undertakes a sensitivity analysis of his geo-economic model, allowing eight key parameters to take on different values and calculating the impact on the model's endogenous variables, such as emissions, temperature increase, warming damage, world output, and so forth.[31] He then recalculates the optimal mitigation policy taking into account these uncertainties. Not surprisingly, and mainly because of significant nonlinearities in the model, the optimal reduction in greenhouse gas emissions and the carbon tax required to achieve it are higher in the presence of these uncertainties than they would be with confident best-guess projections of the future. Concretely, the optimal carbon tax during the 1990s under the uncertain conditions postulated by Nordhaus is $12 a ton, compared with less than $5 a ton under the best-guess projection. With uncertainty, of course, society may learn over time, so that optimal policy may change in response to new knowledge.

What about the possibility of truly disastrous outcomes as a result of global warming? While the scientific community does not put a high probability on them, three catastrophic scenarios are occasionally discussed: (i) sufficient warming to release the extensive methane contained in the arctic permafrost, leading to a strong and possible rapid reinforcement of warming; (ii) sufficient warming to break up the Antarctic ice dam and release great volumes of ice into the ocean, rapidly raising its level several meters, rather than the expected half a meter; and (iii) sufficient glacial melting in Greenland to deflect the warm north Atlantic currents, making Europe a much *colder* place. In terms of figure 1,

31. Nordhaus (1994).

these and other disastrous outcomes could be depicted as schedule 3'—an adaptation to a path 2' that is not shown.

These possibilities, however remote, raise the question of risk aversion and how much insurance societies are willing to buy against improbable but highly costly contingencies. There is no doubt that individuals greatly vary in their degree of risk aversion and that commercial insurance policies do only a modest job of bringing these diverse preferences into harmony. The market for differences in risk preference is much less well developed than the market for differences in time preference. Each society has its own mechanism, through the political process, for deciding on the degree of collective risk aversion. But the mechanism for the world as a whole is even less well developed, being mediated through diplomatic conferences such as those at Rio de Janeiro in 1992.

The political process, while essential for making decisions on collective risk, contains some serious weaknesses, most notably that the discussion is not conducive to honesty and forthrightness. Some risk-averse parties will naturally exaggerate the risks in order to win the support of the less risk averse. Some risk-averse parties will attempt to minimize the estimated costs of early action or suggest that they can be borne by nonvoters (usually corporations). And some parties will use legitimate concerns, such as greenhouse warming, to encourage society to adopt a "life style" more congenial to them—for example, decreasing reliance on the automobile, what for many has been a greatly liberating device. In these last cases, alarms over greenhouse warming become instrumental rather than the true objective.

On the other side, those who expect to bear the costs of political decisions in response to concerns over climate change will tend to minimize the risks and exaggerate the costs of mitigation. In short, everyone should be on guard against misleading or exaggerated arguments from all sides.

International Considerations

Greenhouse warming, like ozone depletion but unlike acid rain, is a global problem, in principle affecting all societies. Similarly, preventive action to be effective must be global, although actions by individual countries can serve to mitigate the greenhouse effect. It is true that in the late twentieth century most fossil fuel consumption takes place in the rich countries of Europe, North America, and Japan, plus the former centrally planned economies. But damaging emissions from deforestation and rice cultivation occur mainly in the developing countries. Moreover, as discussed earlier, developing countries as a group are expected to become major consumers of fossil fuel in the twenty-first century, so their cooperation will eventually become essential if emissions are to be reduced.

Leaders and intellectual elites in developing as well as developed countries are increasingly aware of environmental degradation resulting from human activity—not least because some large urban areas in developing countries have become so environmentally unattractive. But while consciousness of environmental degradation has increased compared with 10 to 20 years ago, other issues still command much more attention. Leaders in developing countries must deal with the fact that the 1980s were not a good decade in terms of economic development. Large external debts continue to weigh heavily on some countries, and a number of governments are politically shaky, in part (but only in part) for economic reasons; some are even embroiled in civil war. These are more pressing issues than the environment, more pressing even than the possibility of dramatic climate change in the next century. In short, most low-income countries have a relatively high social discount rate.

Developing countries are not likely to constrain their economic growth—hence their demand for energy—for the sake of environmental improvement. Furthermore, they argue with some plausibility that apart from local air and water pollution global environmental degradation is perpetrated overwhelmingly by the rich countries, with significant help from the former centrally planned economies. This position is largely correct with respect to present and past conditions; the fact that relative contributions can change markedly with successful economic development is a matter they are likely to consider only after development has occurred.

The bottom line is that many developing countries will co-operate with developed countries in reducing the emission of greenhouse gases so long as it does not require great commitment on their part (mainly in terms of domestic political conflict) and so long as the developed countries incur the extra costs associated with that cooperation, a position that was taken at the Rio conference.

Indeed, developing countries individually and as a group may attempt to extract a price for their cooperation on environmental matters beyond the incremental costs of changing their behavior, to the extent that they detect that the environment has become a priority issue for the developed countries. Developing countries have long felt frustrated over their lack of adequate "bargaining leverage" with respect to the rich countries, many of whom were former colonial powers. This helps to explain the apparently perverse applause that many oil-importing developing countries gave OPEC in 1974 when the oil exporters sharply raised the price of oil. Many saw OPEC as giving developing countries important bargaining leverage. That price increase certainly caught the attention of the developed countries in a way that no previous issue (except wars for independence) had done. In the end, however, it proved to be a weak bargaining weapon, in large part because there was no way to wield it effectively.

Even when the governments of developing countries agree on the desirability of improving the environment, or restraining its deterioration, their priorities are usually elsewhere. It would not be surprising, therefore, to find them trying to extract some quid pro quo for their environmental cooperation. Indeed, UNCED is noteworthy both for the enlargement of its original agenda—from environment toward development—and for the dominance of development issues in the preparatory work for the conference. This work suggested that $125 billion a year in development assistance would be required to carry out the objectives of the conference over the remainder of the 1990s (thus doubling the roughly $60 billion available in 1990), of which less than one-fifth was directed toward environmental issues. The remainder was to be devoted to developmental objectives embodied in Agenda 21, one of the products of the UNCED; yet in the end the developed countries made no commitment with respect to these large sums.[32]

For these reasons, the international negotiating environment for mitigation is likely to be very complicated. One strategy is for the OECD countries to take the assignment upon themselves, in the hope that developing countries will later join the consensus after their incomes and fossil fuel consumption have risen considerably. This strategy does not exclude actions within developing countries, provided the OECD countries are willing to pay for it, perhaps through World Bank loans that are designed with climate change considerations in mind. The problem with this strategy is that there seems to be no right time for a country to graduate from developing to developed status, especially if it is costly. Some countries have resisted the reclassification because they would lose their eligibility for highly concessional IDA loans (from the International Development Agency) and tariff preferences under the Generalized System of Preferences.

Another possible tack would be to allocate "property rights" to the atmosphere for carbon emissions, by analogy with the extension of national economic rights to management of the 200-mile exclusive economic zone in the late 1970s. Since the costs of reducing carbon dioxide will vary greatly from country to country, economic efficiency would be served if these emission rights were tradable—that is, if countries where costs of reducing carbon emissions were high could buy emission rights from countries where costs were low. This idea has attracted much attention from economists.[33] The logically prior step, however, requires allocation of emission rights, and in practice that is likely to prove impossible to do and to enforce. At one end,

32. The developed country parties to the Rio convention did, however, agree to provide financing for greenhouse gas mitigation sufficient to cover the costs of developing countries undertaking such actions, through existing international institutions such as the UN Development Program and the Global Environment Facility administered by the World Bank. Such grants or loans would be conditional on specific actions.

33. One set of estimates suggests that allowing emission rights to be traded would save 0.4 to 0.7 percent of gross world product in the year 2050, reducing the costs (according to the GREEN model) from 2.6 percent to 1.9 percent of gross world product for a 2 percent a year reduction from baseline trajectories across five regions. Organization for Economic Cooperation and Development (1993, p.33).

following historical practice whenever rights are allocated (examples being petroleum or textile imports, price-controlled domestic petroleum, and SO2 emission rights in the United States), emission rights could be issued in proportion to current emissions, uniformly scaled back by the desired amount. That principle of allocation would be completely unacceptable to developing countries, who would see it as thwarting their development objectives and rewarding past miscreancy (even if it was unwitting). Allocation by GDP, which is highly but not perfectly correlated with recent emissions, is unlikely to provide greater appeal to these countries.

At the other extreme, some analysts in developing countries have suggested that emission rights be based on population, thus according China, India, Indonesia, Brazil, Nigeria, Pakistan, and Bangladesh about half of such rights. Such a principle would have the undesirable effect of encouraging population growth. That problem could be dealt with practically by defining rights in terms of population as of a particular date, say, June 1992. But since this is a problem that will mature gradually over the next two centuries, such an allocational principle involves a moral arbitrariness little different from that associated with any other principle.[34] Moreover, allocation according to population faces the possibility, indeed the likelihood, that transfers from rich to highly populated poor countries would be so great that the rich would rather not participate in the scheme: the costs to them would outweigh any likely benefits to them.[35]

34. Moreover, the moral logic of basing rights to atmospheric disposal on population suggests that those rights should be given to individuals. Where government is representative, that allocation perhaps need not be taken literally; but where government is not representative, as in many developing countries, there is no moral case for giving allocations to governments on the basis of the population they rule over.

35. Krause, Bach, and Koomey discuss fair sharing of their proposed 300 billion ton allotment of carbon emissions, noting the fact that most past emissions have come from a small share of the world's population. They conclude that a cumulative per capita allotment would be fair, but also totally impracticable on a global scale. Rough justice is served by dividing the 300 billion ton allotment evenly between industrialized and developing countries. This implies that industrialized countries should achieve a 20 percent reduction in carbon emissions by 2005 and 75 percent by 2035, a very rapid reduction. Krause, Bach, and Koomey (1992, pp. 259, 263). Among the industrialized countries a per capita allotment seems reasonable to the authors. At 1986 emission rates, that leaves 25 years of emissions to the United States, except insofar as it is able to buy surplus allotment from low

Moreover, *any* scheme that involves large unconditional transfers to the governments of developing countries is likely to arouse great skepticism in the rich democracies, quite apart from the fiscal problem of raising the funds to be transferred. Governments of developing countries have not inspired high confidence in their abilities to use foreign capital productively during the past two decades, and the strong inclination in the donor community is to link official transfers to particular projects in the management of which the donors have some role or to make them conditional on policy changes which the donor community feels are necessary for improved economic performance and growth. Any such conditions, however, would undermine the notion of tradable emission rights under consideration here.[36]

Perhaps the most reasonable basis for allocating emission rights and obliging countries to reduce emissions would be to calculate a business-as-usual trajectory of emissions for each country on the basis of recent history, development prospects, and past experience with the evolution of greenhouse gas emissions in relation to economic development. Then each country could be charged with reducing emissions by a uniform percentage (chosen in relation to some measure of global reduction requirements) *relative to the assigned trajectory*. But even if this allocation of rights and responsibilities were accepted as reasonable, the debate would simply shift to the choice of trajectories for each country.

If developing countries cannot be easily persuaded to participate substantially in reducing greenhouse gas emissions through financial incentives, can they be cajoled into doing so through threats? Inevitably when the question of international coordination of policies arises, it brings with it the question of what to do about free-riders or noncompliers, which in turn raises the ques-

---

emitting industrial countries such as Switzerland, France, Sweden, and Japan. Developing countries, on the authors' proposal, would return their emissions to current levels by early next century, having allowed them to rise by about 50 to 100 percent in the next two decades.

36. Tradable emission rights involve a problem of enforceability, since a country selling such rights would have an incentive to "defect" after the sale—that is, not take all the steps to reach its emission targets adjusted for those it had sold. So payments would have to be delayed and conditional on more stringent actions to limit greenhouse gas emissions. But that is different from the conditionality on use of the funds discussed above.

tion of trade sanctions, since few countries are willing to go to war over environmental issues. The issue has already arisen in connection with nonsignatories to and noncompliers with the Montreal and London protocols on the reduction of CFC production and use. Exports of CFCs to such countries were prohibited after 1993, and imports of CFC-containing products were also prohibited. A decision on how to deal with the more complicated question of trade in products that use CFCs in their production (especially electronic products) was deferred. These trade provisions, along with the carrots of financial assistance and technology transfer, may have helped to induce many more developing countries to sign the amended Montreal Protocol in London in 1990 than had agreed to the 1987 protocol. But the disciplinary actions do not go beyond CFCs to encompass more general trade.

It would be difficult to deny imports related to the emission of greenhouse gases without prohibiting trade with the offending country, since CO_2-producing energy is required for virtually all production. Yet prohibiting trade would impose costs not only on the offending countries but also on their trading partners, costs that might well exceed those of greenhouse warming. The advantages of one international regime would be sacrificed for another. Even if the threat worked, in the sense that countries were induced to comply with the emission objectives and the threat did not have to be exercised, its existence might induce some important countries— China comes to mind—to reduce their dependence on trade as a matter of policy and so avoid the possible cost of sanctions in the future. That, too, would represent a cost of compliance.[37]

Even among developed countries there is likely to be serious debate over how costly actions should be shared among countries.[38] This source of contention is present in the best of circum-

37. Threats to reduce trade and aid are used today to influence the behavior of countries, most notably in the development of nuclear weapons and other weapons of mass destruction (and, to some extent, the missiles to deliver them). The day may come when greenhouse warming is widely agreed to be an equal threat to humanity, but that is not yet the case.

38. During the 1979–80 world oil shock, precipitated by the Iranian revolution, the developed countries struggled at the 1979 Economic Summit in Tokyo and subsequently at the International Energy Agency to allocate "fair shares" of demand reduction in the world oil market. With some stipulated exceptions, they finally settled on targets that called for

stances whenever a collective good is involved, since there is no obviously correct principle for burden sharing. Contribution to the problem, ability to pay, and accrual of future benefits all vie for consideration, along with the diverse practical political constraints that countries face. But it is especially a source of contention when ignorance about the nature and distribution of the "good" in question—in this case, the benefits from mitigation actions—is great, as it is at present.

The favorite solution of economists to a negative externality is to tax it (or, equivalently, auction rights to it); and where the externality is global the tax should be global.[39] A uniform global tax on carbon emissions—and the CO_2-equivalent tax on methane and other greenhouse gases—has two major advantages. First, it would encourage the reduction of emissions where it can be done at least cost, since all emitters would have the same incentive to reduce emissions but only those who could save more in carbon tax payments than it cost to reduce carbon emissions would undertake the reductions. Others would simply pay the tax. Second, it would generate revenues for governments that have trouble finding sources of revenue that do not negatively affect economic incentives to work, save, or undertake commercial risks. That should make it attractive to finance ministries everywhere.

However, as recent U.S. experience with a btu-based energy tax illustrates, even modest energy taxes are politically unpopular. The European Commission proposed a somewhat more ambitious tax for energy, raising the tax on oil to the equivalent of about $10 a barrel (roughly 50 percent) by 2000. That tax has yet to be enacted. Moreover, the proposal paradoxically but not surprisingly gave special preference to coal, which is produced at high cost in a number of EC countries and is the most carbon-intensive of the fossil fuels, and would also levy a tax on nuclear power, which is

---

1980 oil imports by each IEA member country (plus France) not to exceed those in 1977 or 1978. But the process was difficult and acrimonious even under what were considered emergency conditions. In the end the targets were comfortably achieved, but through high oil prices and economic slowdown at least as much as through measures adopted specifically to reduce oil imports. See Putnam and Bayne (1987, chap. 8) for a discussion of the 1979 Tokyo Summit and the follow-up actions.

39. See, for example, chapters by John Whalley and Randall Wigle, "The International Incidence of Carbon Taxes," and James M. Poterba, "Tax Policy to Combat Global Warming: On Designing a Carbon Tax," in Dornbusch and Poterba (1991).

the least carbon-intensive major source of energy. In short, a straight carbon emissions tax proved to be politically untenable even before taking it to legislatures.[40]

Two other problems need to be mentioned, neither insuperable. The first concerns the fact that energy (especially oil) was taxed differentially among countries in the early 1990s, and some countries continue to price both coal and oil well below world levels. Should a uniform tax be levied from an uneven initial condition? Ideally not, but if existing pricing practices reflect existing national preferences with respect to each country's authority over the allocation of resources, a case can be made that the *new* carbon tax should be uniform, not the total tax burden on fuels. Of course, national policies would have to be monitored to assure that the effect of the new tax was not undermined by other changes in tax or subsidy policy.[41]

The second problem concerns the disposition of revenue. Current estimates suggest that to adequately affect emissions the tax might have to be substantial. A substantial tax on a major input would generate much revenue. To whom should it accrue? Oil producers will suggest that if oil is to be taxed, they should levy it and get the revenue—indeed, that is what OPEC's attempts to control oil prices amount to.[42] Oil-consuming countries will feel doubly aggrieved if they must charge more for oil to discourage its consumption yet do not get the revenue. They will insist that the tax be levied on consumption and accrue to them.

There is a third possible claimant: the international community. The international community has accepted a number of collective obligations that are cumulatively expensive. Caring for refugees and peacekeeping are only the most apparent. Refugees alone cost

40. In the early 1990s Denmark, Finland, the Netherlands, Norway, and Sweden introduced fuel taxes in the name of greenhouse warming. But except for the Netherlands these taxes have many exemptions, such as the use of fossil fuels for electricity generation, and thus are not based mainly on carbon emissions. Even in the case of the Netherlands, the tax is based half on carbon emissions, half on energy content. Germany continues to subsidize coal production directly, an action hardly consistent with taking carbon emissions seriously. U.S. Department of Energy (1994).

41. Anderson in Anderson and Blackhurst (1992) points out that simply removing the subsidies and price controls that now exist for coal use in many countries would simultaneously increase trade and improve air quality—as well as reducing greenhouse gas emissions—by raising the world price of coal.

42. Indeed, the Rio convention enjoins its parties to "take into consideration" when implementing their policies the adverse effects on those developing countries that are highly dependent on production and export of fossil fuels (article 4.10).

the United Nations about $1 billion in 1992, and peacekeeping operations had run at an annual rate of about $3 billion by the end of that year, of which half was for Cambodia. Special assessments are now made for these activities, with several countries, including Russia and the United States, in arrears. The regular UN budget currently totals more than $1 billion a year. In addition, donor countries finance the United Nations Development Program (UNDP) and IDA (at about $5 billion a year) for economic assistance to the poorest developing countries.[43] In addition, the Rio convention conditions cooperation by developing countries in reducing emissions on new financial support from the rich countries. Some or all of these activities could be financed by revenues from an internationally agreed tax levied on all countries in pursuit of a common objective; obviously the major emitters, currently the rich countries, would pay most of the tax. But as countries develop, their contribution would increase automatically, an attractive feature of such an arrangement.

Estimates from several global energy-environment models suggest that a *uniform* reduction in carbon emissions from a business-as-usual baseline for each country or region would require very different carbon tax rates if that were the policy instrument used to reduce emissions. That result suggests that a uniform tax rate across the regions studied would result in quite different reductions from the baseline—as one would expect from the observation that countries around the world use energy with very different degrees of efficiency. Table 1 reports the carbon tax (in 1990 dollars a ton) that would be required in five regions by the year 2050 to reduce carbon emissions by 2 percent *annually* from the baseline trajectory. Since the baseline trajectories project that energy-related carbon emissions will increase from roughly 6 billion tons a year in 1990 to 11 to 19 billion tons in 2050, the 2 percent annual reduction would reduce emissions to between 3.4 and 5.7 billion tons in 2050, or below the levels of 1990.[44]

Two points are noteworthy about table 1. First, there are large differences among the columns (each reporting a different study), reflecting different assumptions about baseline trajectories, inter-

43. Figures on the UN budget are from *The Europa Year Book 1994* (pp. 9, 43–51).
44. Organization for Economic Cooperation and Development (1993, p. 19).

Table 1. *Tax Required by 2050 to Achieve a 2 Percent Annual Reduction in Carbon Emissions from Baseline Projections*
$1,990 per ton of carbon

	Model			
Region	Edmonds/ Reilly	Manne/ Richels	GREEN	Carbon rights trade model
United States	1,096	208	340	754
Other OECD	734	208	299	365
Former Soviet Union	325	990	180	2,245
China	341	240	67	1,109
Rest of world	1,012	727	329	763

Source: Organization for Economic Cooperation and Development (1993, p. 153).

energy and factor substitution possibilities, energy-saving technical change, and the presence of a non-carbon-emitting backstop source of energy. So at this stage there is little agreement on the costs of reducing emissions by an agreed amount.

Second, in each of the studies there are substantial variations in the required carbon tax across the regions, reflecting markedly different opportunities for reduction of carbon emissions. That suggests that global economic efficiency calls for diverse responses across regions, keyed to a common "shadow price" for carbon emissions. (Full efficiency would impose analogous charges on production of methane—from, say, rice and cattle—and other greenhouse gases, which are not included in the studies reported here). Countries that cut more would of course pay less tax.

By 2050, the world price of oil (in 1990 dollars), 56 percent carbon by weight, is assumed to be $50 a barrel, more than two times the current price; the price of coal, 75 percent carbon by weight, is assumed to be $60 a ton, about 50 percent above the current price at points of importation (that is, not at the mine). Thus, a tax of $208 per ton of carbon in 2050 would represent a 31 percent tax on oil at that time and a 260 percent tax on coal.[45] The loss in GDP engendered by this program ranges (across the studies) from 1.3 percent to 4.9 percent in 2050 for the United

45. Author's calculations using data from Organization for Economic Cooperation and Development (1993, pp. 14, 135, 153).

States, from 2.3 to 6.4 percent for the former Soviet Union, and from 2.1 to 5.1 percent for the rest of the world (today's developing countries, minus China).[46] These results should be regarded as exploratory rather than definitive, but even the low estimates suggest a substantial cost to bringing energy-related CO_2 emissions below 1990 levels. As noted above, permitting trade in emission rights among regions—a uniform carbon tax achieves the same result—would reduce these costs but still leave them substantial.

The revenue these taxes would raise is also substantial. For instance, a $208 tax per ton of carbon in the United States (the lowest rate reported in table 1) would raise nearly $300 billion in revenue, 1.8 percent of 2050 GDP. A $329 tax per ton in the rest of the world would raise $610 billion in 2050, nearly 3.2 percent of rest-of-world GDP in that year.[47]

International cooperation in other fields has progressed most successfully when there was agreement not only on the objective but also on how best to achieve it. As suggested by the prolonged and sometimes acrimonious history leading to international cooperation in the containment of contagious diseases, hardly a controversial objective, the absence of scientific consensus on key aspects of how greenhouse gas emissions translate into global temperature changes, and on how those temperature changes will affect the human condition, will make it difficult to agree on how to share costly actions, or indeed on what actions should be taken.[48] Large differences in assessments of the costs of mitigation will simply magnify the difficulties.

Moreover, some countries may be expected to benefit from at least a modest amount of warming. In Russia, for example, the weather might become *less* uncertain, with more moisture expected in the grain-growing areas. This possibility may also induce reluctance to contribute to an international effort.

These various considerations will tend to push countries away from mitigating actions toward reliance on adaptation, where the actions are in response to identifiable localized problems—a shore being inundated or croplands being flooded—and where the ex-

46. Organization for Economic Cooperation and Development (1993, p. 157).
47. Author's calculations using data from Organization for Economic Cooperation and Development (1993, pp. 19, 21, 145, 153, 157).
48. Cooper and others (1989).

penditures are willingly made by the direct beneficiaries. Even foreign aid in this case can be focused on well-defined mitigation of visible hardship, a factor that makes garnering foreign support easier. In short, the demands on international cooperation will be much less acute with a broad strategy of adaptation than they would be with a major commitment to mitigation.

Implications for U.S. Policy

The low prospect for international cooperation arises partly because of high uncertainty about the character, magnitude, and regional impact of climate change, especially as developing countries have more urgent priorities. This fact suggests that policy should emphasize reducing the cone of uncertainty, that is, it should stress a major global research effort, focusing on understanding of important ocean-atmosphere interactions, locating the "missing" carbon emitted over the past two centuries, and the determinants of sun-reflecting cloud formation. Before being taken seriously for the future, large-scale climate models should be improved so that they can indicate *past* climate satisfactorily. A workable international consensus on the dangers mankind faces is necessary for serious, costly collaboration to avert those dangers.

Beyond that, high-income industrial countries can take steps to reduce their emissions of greenhouse gases. Action to reduce ozone depletion has already taken place. These countries have experienced much improvement over the past twenty years in achieving more efficient use of energy, having been jolted out of complacency by the first oil shock. But much further improvement is possible, even without new technology. Low-cost government strategies can encourage greater energy efficiency through providing information (for example, in the schools), removing regulatory impediments (for example, in building codes and regulated utility pricing formulas), and imposing modest tax increases on energy, producing welcome revenue.[49] Research on new, noncarbon sources of energy should also be pursued.

49. For greater detail, see National Academy of Sciences (1991) and Cooper in Hurrell and Kingsbury (1992).

Taking costly actions that induce major changes in life-style on grounds of climate change would be premature and ineffective in any case without extensive international cooperation. National emissions targets must be viewed as a device, not especially effective, for focusing attention on the issue, rather than as comprising a policy.

Energy use is still "subsidized"—that is, sold well below world prices—in many parts of the world, especially China, Russia, and many oil-exporting countries, resulting in excessive use. These countries should be encouraged, or induced through conditions on international loans, to commit to the goal of raising their energy prices over time, while we await harder information on the dynamics of potential climate change.

Chapter 6

Conclusions

THIS book discusses the possible need for international action with respect to traditional natural resources and with respect to more recent environmental concerns. If one accepts the long-established allocation of property to the territorial nation-state, one can conclude that there is no distinctively international problem for nationally owned resources, except for global disturbances that may arise in connection with worldwide shortages, real or contrived, of key commodities—in practice, petroleum and food grain. The proper response there, which has been imperfectly implemented with respect to oil, is to provide for international stockpiles of the critical commodities, with agreed criteria for releasing the commodities to reduce high prices (the manifestation of scarcity).

Local ecologies, if thought to contain potentially valuable species, can be purchased and protected under the laws of most countries, although in some developing countries ownership of the land is limited to citizens. That that is done to only a limited extent may reflect some institutional barriers, but it may reflect the judgment by the major users (mostly pharmaceutical companies) that the expected future value of the species involved does not justify the costs of purchasing and protecting them. Genetic material, particularly from plants, can be collected and preserved in locations away from the natural ecological setting. These remarks do not deny, however, that some natural environments are being needlessly destroyed because of defects in both policies and markets.

Where valuable resources are not nationally owned, they can be exploited too rapidly and too extensively because no one has adequate incentive to husband them for future use. This phenomenon has been most evident with the harvesting of ocean creatures—some whales and fish. Inaccessibility and the high cost of exploitation are the major protections for common property—outer space, Antarctica, the deep seabed in the late twentieth century, and oceans in the past. But advancing technology will gradually change that, as it has done with fisheries. The international community has tentatively installed international regimes to deal with these commons. They variously involve laissez faire, with respect to outer space, subject to certain prohibitions; first-come first-served, with respect the electromagnetic spectrum and geostationary orbits, subject to notification and certain rules limiting interference with the activities of others; limited access for Antarctica and whaling; and national appropriation for coastal fisheries and offshore oil.

Environmental issues typically involve "externalities": unwelcome imposition on what others consider to be their rights. If these externalities remain strictly within each nation, and if each nation has a political system that permits residents to register their preferences with respect to environmental externalities, no specifically international issue is posed. This proposition presumes that each national community has a right to define and pursue its own objectives. Of course such national decisions may affect other countries through foreign trade, just as decisions with respect to national saving and investment, education, dispute settlement, and a host of other issues involving laws and social structure may affect patterns of trade. That is no reason to regard the actions (or lack of actions) as suspect. Indeed, trade permits different communities to enjoy their diverse preferences and circumstances at a higher standard of living than they could do in isolation.

Rapid changes in environmental rules, like rapid changes in any other important circumstance, can cause dislocations to production in the community experiencing such changes. Such dislocation can sometimes be reduced through coordinated international action if all relevant communities wish to move in the same direction.

If the environmental externalities are regional in nature, as is often the case with water use and river and air pollution, downwind or downstream neighbors will have a direct interest in the activities of other countries. Here binational or regional action is required, but not action at the global level. There are many such examples—involving not only river use and air pollution but also dumping of waste at sea and management of regional coastal fisheries. Such examples of cooperation range from great successes to dismal failures.

A few externalities are global in their impact. Radioactive fallout from nuclear testing was one that was recognized early and that led to the atmospheric test ban treaty between the United States and the Soviet Union in 1963. (France and China, however, declined to join.) Short-wave radio broadcasts, which may interfere with one another, have been subject to international reporting and conflict resolution for many decades. Different band-widths have been allocated to different purposes (such as marine, police, or ham-radio communication) internationally to minimize interference.

More recently, the international community has become concerned with depletion of stratospheric ozone, which provides a protective shield against ultraviolet radiation, traced to the long-lived man-made CFCs used widely since the 1930s for a variety of domestic and industrial purposes. Agreement was reached in 1990 among the developed countries to phase out production and consumption of CFCs altogether by 2000; developing countries were urged to join in the ban, and many of them agreed, but were given a ten-year grace period. Agreement was facilitated by rapidly converging scientific evidence on the ozone-destroying effects of CFCs, as well as by the development of not-too-costly substitutes for CFCs in most of their uses—based on company research partly induced by concern with the global effects of CFCs, a good example of induced technical change. It remains to be seen whether all parties will comply with the agreement and whether, in turn, the ozone layer will begin to rebuild.

Potentially the most portentous issue involving global externalities arises from the emission of greenhouse gases—carbon dioxide,

a product of combustion, being quantitatively the most important—on a scale that may be sufficiently great to increase the
average temperature of the earth's surface and thereby alter global
climate patterns. The nature of such alterations is highly uncertain
at this stage and could even be beneficial to some regions. Yet, they
carry the potential for substantial harm to communities as they
function today. Climate change is likely to take place slowly, however, so its effects will become known only gradually, and most
communities may find adaptation to the altered circumstances
relatively easy. On the other hand, the potential for serious damage
to some human communities and to natural ecological systems has
led a number of observers to favor action in the relatively near
future to reduce greenhouse gas emissions substantially.

Such a move, to be effective, would call for a high degree of
international cooperation, resulting in skillfully executed national
policies to provide households and firms with the right rules and
incentives to alter deeply entrenched patterns of behavior, involving mainly consumption of energy provided by fossil fuels but also
important agricultural practices. Since greenhouse gas emissions
anywhere have potential global effects but reducing them would
involve fundamental changes in the way economies have func-
tioned for the past century, every country has an incentive to
encourage other countries to act boldly while undertaking only
modest actions itself.

The situation is further complicated by the fact that many
developing countries have begun to grow rapidly, and others see
the prospect of doing so. Rapid growth historically has been associated with a rapid increase in consumption of energy; but because
growth and development are far higher priorities than the avoidance of global climate change, particularly when the problem can
be traced to the developed countries, developing countries are
reluctant to sign on. To engage them in high-cost actions to reduce
greenhouse gas emissions will require some carrots in the form of
financial assistance and transfer of technology and sticks in the
form of threatened reductions in foreign aid and trade.

The problem is further complicated by the fact that to be
effective an international agreement must not merely achieve agree-

ment on the reduction in greenhouse gases and how those reductions should be distributed among countries, but it must be continually policed because of an ever-present incentive for each country, and for households and firms within countries, to increase its emissions while others keep them down. In short, the demands on international cooperation are extreme.

These demands might be met given a clear and present danger. But the uncertainties surrounding global climate change, the impact of such change on various nations, and the costs of adjusting to those changes are so great as to make agreement on a program of action at the global level impossible.

Under these circumstances, the Framework Convention on Climate Change of 1992 was a remarkable achievement. True, it committed developing countries to nothing beyond acknowledging the problem and cooperating in research and information gathering, provided these cost them nothing. But it committed the developed countries to introducing actions that would reduce greenhouse gas emissions (other than CFCs) to 1990 levels in the relatively near future, to framing their policies with the problem of climate change in mind, and to creating institutional and financial mechanisms to help developing countries reduce their emissions. Since at present emissions can probably be reduced at lower cost in many developing countries (and in the formerly centrally planned economies of eastern Europe), the rich countries have some incentive to facilitate those developments. The convention permits developed countries to get credit for reductions in emissions that they facilitate and finance in other countries. Such crediting would be easier in the context of clear national targets for greenhouse gas emissions, but national communities are not yet sufficiently convinced of the urgency of the problem and the feasibility of solutions to accept formal targets, which in any case raise a host of distributional issues that the international community is not yet prepared to face.

Comments

Kym Anderson

THIS is a clearly argued and deceptively nontechnical paper—deceptive in the sense that it is easy to read and yet embodies a huge amount of economics and political economy. It is spiced with well-chosen examples to illustrate the range of issues that fall under the rubric of international conflict and cooperation in natural resource and environmental management.

The study begins, appropriately, by dismissing the notion that the world is running out of natural resources. It does so by pointing to the roles of technological improvements and economic incentives in altering effective resource supplies and quantities demanded. While those with a doomsday mentality may remain unconvinced, the evidence presented by Richard Cooper shows clearly that, with respect to resources, the world as a whole is being sustainably managed in the sense of the Brundtland Commission's definition of development—that is, not compromising the ability of future generations to meet their needs. Cooper notes, for example, that global investments well exceed the global sales of natural resources. One could add that even if attention is confined to resource supplies alone, the current stock of known mineral and energy reserves is higher now than a quarter century ago, despite the fact that during the

Kym Anderson is director of the Centre for International Economic Studies, University of Adelaide.

75

past 25 years the world has consumed more than the known reserves of the late 1960s.[1]

Cooper then moves on to three other sets of issues: (i) use of the global commons; (ii) effects on national actions on other nations' citizens via markets; and (iii) effects of national actions on other nations' citizens via environmental externalities. Let me say a little about each.

The global commons (resources not yet allocated to national states) primarily include the oceans, outer space, and, somewhat controversially, Antarctica. A key question raised in this section of the paper is the extent to which these should be jointly managed rather than partitioned to nation states and managed through property rights. If the latter were to dominate, it immediately raises North-South issues, as arose about a decade ago during discussions about mining the ocean seabed. If joint management dominates, problems can arise if some of the management objectives are more widely supported than others. In the study, whaling is used to illustrate this problem. In that case, the objective of efficient harvesting is more widely shared than that of animal welfare. The 1985 moratorium on whaling was broken in 1993 by Norway because its government believed that minke whale numbers had recovered sufficiently for a limited harvest to be possible without endangering the species, while other governments feel strongly that the moratorium should continue. A more extreme set of examples, and one mentioned little in the paper, has to do with certain species deemed at risk of extinction (such as elephants). That concern has led to trade bans under the Convention on International Trade in Endangered Species (CITES) that are not only inefficient but, ironically, may even put the elephant and its environment at greater risk.[2]

The next category of issues discussed in the paper involves the effect on international competitiveness of differences across countries in national environmental standards (in the absence of externalities). If country A has stricter standards than country B for pollution from a particular production process, producers in country A feel aggrieved at their loss of competitiveness. Yet country B's

1. Beckerman (1992).
2. See, for example, Barbier and others (1990).

lower emission standards may simply reflect a lower population density, a lower per capita income, or a less strong preference for clean air.[3] These determinants of country B's competitiveness do not much differ from other determinants of comparative advantage. If that point could only be accepted, there would be fewer disputes in the absence in international externalities—just as there would be fewer disputes among nations over labor standards, competition policy, and tax policy if the mutual recognition rule were accepted.

But disputes *do* arise, because some people's sensibilities are offended by that mutual recognition rule. The recent U.S.-Mexican controversy over tuna fishing with dolphin-unfriendly nets is mentioned as a case in point; it resulted in a ban on U.S. imports of all Mexican tuna, which Mexico protested under the GATT. Why did the GATT panel side with Mexico? One reason is that not to do so would have greatly increased the risk of more countries using trade threats to impose their view of appropriate environmental policy on other countries. That would be an undesirable development not just because it smacks of environmental imperialism but also because those other countries would retaliate with their own trade barriers, thus unraveling the trade liberalizations achieved in previous rounds of multilateral trade negotiations. Another reason GATT did not support the U.S. position was that superior solutions existed. These included the labeling of cans as dolphin-friendly (which would apply equally to U.S. and imported products) and negotiating a compromise. The latter resulted in U.S. monitors now being permitted on Mexican fishing boats. Even so, this episode has been very costly in terms of reinforcing the view of many environmental groups that GATT is unfriendly to the environment.

As a consequence, GATT-contracting parties are now more wary of bringing such issues before a GATT dispute settlement panel, at least during the fragile 1994–95 ratification period of the Uruguay Round and transformation of the GATT Secretariat into the World Trade Organization (WTO). A case in point is

3. There is a growing body of empirical evidence that supports the view that environmental standards tend to rise with per capita income, at least after upper-middle-income status is reached. In addition, to the Grossman and Krueger (1993) paper mentioned by Cooper, see also the more recent paper by Grossman (1994).

the threat by the United States to impose trade sanctions on imports of Norwegian fish in response to Norway's resuming fishing of minke whales. Despite the fact that such an import restriction would violate the trade rights of Norway under the GATT, bringing the matter to dispute settlement in the WTO's fist year would be highly inflammatory.

The fourth and final category of issues discussed in the paper has to do with situations involving environmental spillovers, where one country's actions affect the environment of some or all other countries. Where spillovers simply involve neighbors, negotiated settlements can be relatively straightforward, although less so the larger the gap between the countries' perceptions of the net benefits of abatement. Moreover, moral hazard problems arise when, for example, a downwind rich country like Japan pays an upwind poor country like China to install stack scrubbers in coal-burning plants: the incentive for China to install such equipment at its own expense and initiative is reduced by Japan's preparedness to pay. And likewise with Sweden paying Poland to pollute less.

The far more complicated situation has to do with global environmental problems—such as ozone depletion and global climate change. As it happens, the Montreal Protocol agreement to phase out the use of chlorofluorocarbons, and so ease ozone depletion, has been remarkably successful. But that is only because the situation had some extremely favorable characteristics: it involved low-cost items, namely, CFCs and halons; they were used mainly in the relatively small number of rich countries; few producers were involved; and the main producer was well advanced in developing a substitute, which, while more expensive, could be marketed earlier and more profitably the sooner CFCs were phased out.[4] Thus all the ingredients favored a quick resolution. As it happened, trade provisions were included in the protocol both as a carrot, to entice signatures, and as a stick, to penalize nonsignatories. The fact that it has not run afoul of the GATT should be mentioned, because it is a counterexample of the claim that trade laws dominate environmental ones: complaints by GATT-contracting parties would be required before it became a problem, and that has not happened.

4. Anderson and Blackhurst (1992, chap. 7).

By contrast to CFC reduction, reducing carbon emissions, methane production, and deforestation so as to slow global warming will be a far greater task. The paper sensibly questions (i) whether global warming is occurring to a significant degree and (ii) whether that is necessarily a bad and costly thing. Even if warming is occurring and will be costly, Cooper presents a strong case for relying on adaptation to climate change rather than trying to mitigate it. Among other things, he provides a long list of reasons why developing countries would be unlikely to join an agreement to mitigate, at least in the absence of substantial bribes or threats. But even agreement among developed countries would be difficult to reach. There is already evidence of considerable difference in their attitudes toward the issue, in the form of large differences in countries' fuel tax rates. Cooper therefore suggests, correctly in my view, that a major international commitment to mitigation is unlikely when there is no immediate danger and the scope for gradual adaptation is considerable.

It might be possible, however, to make some progress on this issue of carbon emissions and at the same time improve real incomes, thus reducing the clash between environmentalists and the GATT. The perception by environmentalists that the GATT and its trade liberalization agenda is environmentally unfriendly might be altered if it were demonstrated that multilateral trade negotiations can lead to changes that improve not only real incomes but also the environment.[5] One such possibility arose at the end of the Uruguay Round, whereby the European Union (EU) agreed to make "best endeavours" to reduce its coal production subsidies and associated coal import restrictions. If user prices in the EU remain unchanged but coal producer subsidies there are lowered, the increased imports of coal would raise the international price of this fuel, thereby reducing its use in the rest of the world and encouraging a substitution toward (it is hoped) cleaner fuels. And an incidental bonus would be a reduction in acid rain in Europe, insofar as imported

5. Another positive contribution the GATT-WTO could play is in monitoring trade-related environmental measures (TREMs) if contracting parties, via the now-activated Working Group on Trade and the Environment, agree to formally notify the secretariat of the TREMs as and when they are introduced.

coal has a lower sulphur content.[6] The extent to which this could affect global carbon emissions and provide a free lunch is currently being investigated as part of an OECD-sponsored project using three different global simulation models (Alan Mann's, Warwick McKibbin's, and the OECD's own GREEN model).

As for excessive carbon emissions from the burning of low-quality coal in developing countries, such as India, China, and those in Eastern Europe and the former Soviet Union, a contribution could be played by agencies like the World Bank, in its usual role of making loans conditional on sound economic policy. In this case, that would involve insisting that the artificially low user price of coal be raised toward the international level.

The attention given to carbon emissions is understandable in discussions about global warming, but about a quarter of the contribution to the problem is believed to be shared equally by methane production and deforestation. The paper mentions in passing the methane contribution of rice production and livestock farming but neither they nor the forestry sector is considered when contemplating solutions. One way to draw attention to this would be to include agriculture and forestry in the quantitative global models used to evaluate options, since it may be cheaper to pay developing countries to slow deforestation or to reforest, allowing slower tax increases on fossil fuels. Such dynamic computable general equilibrium models could also be useful for evaluating the environmental effects of multilateral trade agreements—particularly for persuading agnostics and skeptics that (i) even taking into account any adverse environmental effects, trade liberalization is beneficial and (ii) the estimated global benefits of trade reform are often greater, not smaller, when there is proper accounting for the environment.

6. For more on the potential environmental as well as economic benefits that could result from coal trade liberalization, see chapter 8 of Anderson and Blackhurst (1992).

John Whalley

This is a well-written book containing a wealth of useful information. It evaluates the rationale for international policy action in areas related to natural resources and associated transnational issues. It divides the use of natural resources into four separate categories—national use of natural resources, "common heritage" resources, external consequences from national actions not involving transborder externalities, and external consequences from national actions involving transborder externalities—and examines rationales for international action in each. The second and fourth of these receive the most attention: Antarctica, outer space, the ocean seabed, the oceans, and the atmosphere under the former; and ozone depletion and climate change under the latter. Richard Cooper's main task is to ask which cases require international action when natural resource issues are concerned.

My reactions to the study are, first, that it may adopt a more complex classification than really needed for what are essentially simple questions. Second, the relationship between natural resources and the evolution of the world economy could be more fully discussed. And third, there are aspects of the form that such actions should take and how they should be implemented that deserve more emphasis.

It seems to me that the underlying economics here are adequately covered by the general theory of externalities. While the international dimension discussed primarily relates to externalities spanning national borders, where for one reason or another externalities are not internalized, the economics are the same. Thus, whether it is the Montreal Protocol's curb on the use of CFCs, or proposals to reduce carbon emissions through carbon taxes, or concerns over deforestation, the objective of policy is the same—internalization of a noninternalized externality. This is as true of the category labeled common heritage as it is of the others. The category that covers the national use of natural resources is the only one in which no international externality arises since, by definition, internalization on a country-by-country basis already occurs. The more detailed categorization adds relatively little in my

John Whalley is professor of economics, University of Western Ontario.

view. Also, the analytical categories do not seem clearly delineated. For instance, the economic difference between external consequences that involve transborder externalities and those that do is minor; the issue is whether the government in one country can usefully take action when another government is unwilling to internalize the externality.

My second point is that the study could usefully deal with natural resource issues as part of the wider research project into the integration of national economies. Through recent history, certain economies, such as those in Scandinavia, Canada, and Australia, have been seen as resource-based economies. They have typically gone through a series of booms and busts, but the resources exported have traditionally been viewed as a central factor in growth. With the movement toward information-based technologies, the resource requirements of technologically led growth, compared with those of manufacturing-led growth, provide an uncertain future for the more resource-based economies. A further issue is the relationship among resources, environment, and the trade barriers erected to curb the environmental ill-effects of resource trade. For example, the proposed bans on imports of tropical lumber will have major effects on resource trade, and the environmental implications of such trade are not inseparable from issues involving the integration of the world economy. Thus, the paper could better address how resources will be central to international trade in the future. Where are resources likely to come from in future decades? From traditional large suppliers, such as Canada and Russia, or other economies? Moreover, the analysis might ask which rules should apply to trade in the resources.

My third point is that the analysis could have discussed more fully the form that international environmental action should take, as well as developing a rationale for such action.[1] Where externalities are not internalized, there are interesting questions as to the path that the international policy regime should follow. These

1. Although the rationale is the lack of internalization of externalities, it should be noted that in a restricted number of cases international externalities are now being internalized through bilateral deals of the Coase type. One example is the arrangement between Sweden and Poland on acid rain: Sweden is to pay for the installation of emission control equipment in Poland, whose emissions affect Sweden.

questions also relate to the integration of the world economy, as well as to the evolution of global institutions in related areas such as international trade.

The global environmental treaties that have emerged thus far, because they have focused on how to internalize transnational externalities, have a structure different from trade treaties. Take, for example, the Montreal Protocol. In this case, a group of countries jointly committed to terminate their use of CFCs, as well as to ban the production processes that use them and the products that contain them. A schedule of dates was agreed for various joint actions. The difficulty was that a number of countries refused to commit to the agreement, partly because of the obvious benefits of free-riding. To deal with free-riders, parties to the protocol adopted trade sanctions against nonsignatories. Some people now think that an eventual carbon treaty may well go the same way.

Countries that wish to agree on the reduction of other emissions may be confronted with the same problem of how to penalize free-riders. This may lead to further conflicts between existing institutional arrangements outside the environmental arena—such as trade actions that are incompatible with GATT. The design issues thus touch on the form that environmental treaties should take and how to enforce compliance with globally agreed targets through the treaties.

A related issue is that of property rights and the associated questions of compensation. Following UNCED, one cannot help but be struck by the growing North-South divide on environmental issues and protests from the South of green imperialism and eco-imperialism. Their argument is that the South is being asked to truncate their growth and development in order to provide environmental benefits to the North—or, put more simply, to restrain deforestation even though the North chopped down its trees some 200 years ago and subsequently industrialized. Rather than face trade sanctions to enforce Northern objectives, the South argues that it should be compensated for policies that mitigate environmental damage. For example, countries like Malaysia have offered to keep a certain amount of land forested in return for compensation from the North. In other words, the issue is whether resources are global communal property or national property. If the latter, then the developing countries argue that they should be able to use those resources to grow, just as the now industrialized countries did a century ago.

The design of international arrangements and their enforcement thus seems as equally central to integrating national economies as the rationale for international action. Where externalities spanning national borders are not internalized, there is presumably an efficiency rationale for internalization. How that is to be achieved is a core task facing policymakers in the next few years.

References

Anderson, Kym, and Richard Blackhurst, eds. 1992. *The Greening of World Trade Issues.* Ann Arbor, Mich.: University of Michigan Press.

Arnaudo, Raymond V. 1993. "The Antarctic Treaty Is an International Success." *North-South* 2(February–March):7–10.

Barbier, E., and others. 1990. *Elephants, Economics and Ivory.* London: Earthscan.

Beckerman, W. 1992. "Economic Growth and the Environment: Whose Growth? Whose Environment?" *World Development* 20(April): 481–96.

Benedick, Richard E. 1991. *Ozone Diplomacy: New Directions in Safeguarding the Planet.* Cambridge, Mass.: Harvard University Press.

Bureau of the Census. 1992. *Statistical Abstract of the United States.* Washington: U.S. Department of Commerce.

Burk, Dan L., Kenneth Barovsky, and Gladys H. Monroy. 1993. "Biodiversity and Biotechnology." *Science* 260 (June 25): 1900–01.

Busuttil, S., and others, eds. 1990. *Our Responsibilities Towards Future Generations: A Programme of UNESCO and the International Environment Institute.* Malta: Foundation for International Studies.

Charnovitz, Steve. 1992. "GATT and the Environment: Examining the Issues." *International Environmental Affairs* 4(Summer): 203–33.

Cline, William R. 1992. *The Economics of Global Warming.* Washington: Institute for International Economics.

Cooper, Richard N., and others. 1989. *Can Nations Agree? Issues in International Cooperation.* Washington: Brookings.

Corrigan, Richard. 1985. "Haves and Have-Nots Are Competing for a Piece of Ring Around Earth." *National Journal* 17(October 26): 2406–12.

Dornbusch, Rudiger, and James M. Poterba, eds. 1991. *Global Warming:Economic Policy Responses.* Cambridge, Mass.: MIT Press.

Esty, Daniel C. 1994. *Greening the GATT: Trade, Environment, and the Future.* Washington: Institute for International Economics.

Europa Year Book 1994. Rochester, Kent (U.K.): Europa Publications, Ltd.

Fletcher, Lehman B., ed. 1992. *World Food in the 1990s: Production, Trade, and Aid.* Boulder: Westview Press.

Gardner, Richard N. 1992. *Negotiating Survival: Four Priorities After Rio.* New York: Council on Foreign Relations.

General Agreement on Tariffs and Trade (GATT). 1993. *International Trade 1993: Statistics.* Geneva.

Grossman, Gene. 1994. "Pollution and Growth: What Do We Know?" In *The Economics of Sustainable Development,* edited by I. Goldon and L. A. Winters. Cambridge: Cambridge University Press (forthcoming).

————, and Alan B. Krueger. 1993. "Environmental Impacts of a North American Free Trade Agreement." In *The Mexico-US Free Trade Agreement,* edited by Peter Garber. Cambridge, Mass.: MIT Press.

Haas, Peter M., Robert O. Keohane, and Marc A. Levy, eds. 1993. *Institutions for the Earth: Sources of Effective International Environmental Protection.* Cambridge, Mass.: MIT Press.

Hollick, Ann L. and Richard N. Cooper. 1991. "Global Commons: Can They Be Managed?" Working Paper 91-7. Cambridge, Mass.: Center for International Affairs, Harvard University (Spring).

Horowitz, Donald L. 1994. "Democracy in Divided Societies." *Securing Peace in the New Era: Politics in the Former Soviet Union and the Challenge to American Security.* Queenstown, Md.: Aspen Institute.

Horwich, George, and David Leo Weimer, eds. 1988. *Responding to International Oil Crises.* Washington: American Enterprise Institute.

Hufbauer, Gary C., and Jeffrey J. Schott. 1992. *North American Free Trade: Issues and Recommendations.* Washington: Institute for International Economics.

Hurrell, Andrew, and Benedict Kingsbury, eds. 1992. *The International Politics of the Environment: Actors, Interests, and Institutions.* Oxford: Clarendon Press.

International Energy Agency. 1992. *Climate Change Policy Initiatives.* Paris: Organisation for Economic Cooperation and Development.

Jackson, John H. 1992. "World Trade Rules and Environmental Policies: Congruence or Conflict?" *Washington and Lee Law Review* 49 (Fall): 1227–78.

Jaffe, Adam B., and others. 1993. "Environmental Regulation and International Competitiveness: What Does the Evidence Tell Us?" Working Paper R93-42. Kennedy School of Government, Harvard University (December).

Kay, David A., and Harold K. Jacobson. 1983. *Environmental Protection: The International Dimension.* Totowa, N.J.: Allanheld, Osmun.

Kearney, Adam. 1992. "Frozen Assets: Antarctic Minerals Issue Far from Resolution." *Harvard International Review* 15(Fall): 38–40.

Krause, Florentin, Wilfred Bach, and Jonathan Koomey. 1992. *Energy Policy in the Greenhouse.* New York: John Wiley & Sons.

Manne, Alan S., and Richard G. Richels. 1992. *Buying Greenhouse Insurance: The Economic Costs of Carbon Dioxide Emission Limits.* Cambridge, Mass.: MIT Press.

National Academy of Sciences. 1991. *Policy Implications of Greenhouse Warming.* Report of committee chaired by Daniel Evans. Washington: National Academy Press.

Nordhaus, William D. 1992. "Lethal Model 2: The Limits to Growth Revisited." *Brookings Papers on Economic Activity* 2:1992, pp. 1–59.

————. 1994. *Managing the Global Commons: The Economics of Climate Change.* Cambridge, Mass.: MIT Press.

Oliveira-Martins, Joaquim, and others. 1992. "The Costs of Reducing CO_2 Emissions: A Comparison of Carbon Tax Curves with GREEN." Economics Department Working Papers No. 118. Paris: Organisation for Economic Cooperation and Development.

Organization for Economic Cooperation and Development. 1991. *Responding to Climate Change: Selected Economic Issues.* Paris: Organisation for Economic Cooperation and Development.

————. 1993. *The Costs of Cutting Carbon Emissions: Results from Global Models,* edited by Andrew Dean and Peter Hoeller. Paris: Organisation for Economic Cooperation and Development.

Peterson, D. J. 1993. *Troubled Lands; the Legacy of Soviet Environmental Destruction.* Boulder: Westview Press.

Pöhl, Gerhard, and Dubravko Mihaljek. 1989. "Project Evaluation in Practice." Unpublished paper. World Bank (December).

Psacharopoulos, George. 1985. "Returns to Education: A Further International Update and Implications." *Journal of Human Resources* 20 (Fall): 583–604.

Putnam, Robert D., and Nicholas Bayne. 1987. *Hanging Together: Cooperation and Conflict in the Seven-Power Summits,* rev. edition. Cambridge, Mass.: Harvard University Press.

Solow, Robert. 1992. "An Almost Practical Step Toward Sustainability." Fortieth Anniversary Lecture at Resources for the Future, Washington (October).

Stone, Christopher D. 1993. *The Gnat is Older than Man: Global Environment and Human Agenda.* Princeton, N.J.: Princeton University Press.

Waller, Deborah Cook. 1989. "Death of a Treaty: the Decline and Fall of the Antarctic Minerals Convention." *Vanderbilt Journal of International Law* 22: 631–68.

Weintraub, Sidney. 1990. *A Marriage of Convenience: Relations between Mexico and the United States.* New York: Oxford University Press.

Weitzman, Martin. 1992. "On Diversity." *Quarterly Journal of Economics* 107 (May): 363–405.

Wigley, T.M.L., and S.C.B. Raper. 1991. "Detection of the Enhanced Greenhouse Effect on Climate." *Proceedings of the Second World Climate Conference* Cambridge: Cambridge University Press.

Wilson, Edward O. 1992. *The Diversity of Life.* Cambridge, Mass.: Harvard University Press.

World Bank. 1992. *World Development Report, 1992: Development and the Environment.* Oxford: Oxford University Press.

World Commission on Environment and Development. 1987. *Our Common Heritage.* New York: Oxford University Press.

Young, Oran R., and Gail Osherenko, eds. 1993. *Polar Politics: Creating International Environmental Regimes.* Ithaca: Cornell University Press.

Index

Framework Convention on Climate Change of *1992*, 2, 42–43, 55, 57, 64, 73
France, 33; Antarctica and, 12, 14, 16; nuclear testing and, 71; ocean seabed and, 21, 22
Free-riders, 60–61, 83
Full social cost, 30

General Agreement on Tariffs and Trade (GATT), xiii, xvi, xxi, 25, 77, 77–78, 79, 83
Generalized System of Preferences, 58
Genetic material, 7–8, 69
Geostationary orbits, 17–18, 70
German Democratic Republic, 13
Germany: Antarctica and, 13; ocean seabed and, 21
Glacial melting, 41, 54
Global climate change, xvii, 27, 38, 41–53, 67–68, 71–73, 78, 79–80, 81; adaptation to, 47–49, 52, 79; discount rate in, 48–51, 53–54, 56; income and, 46–48; international considerations in, 55–67; mitigation of, 46–55, 62, 66, 79, 83; principal causes of, 43; risk aversion and, 53–55
Global commons. *See* Common heritage (global commons)
Global externalities, 37–38, 71
Grains, 7
Greece, 42
Greenhouse gas emissions. *See* Global climate change
Green imperialism, 83
Greenland, 54
GREEN model, 80
Gross domestic product (GDP), 49, 59, 65, 66
Gross national product (GNP), 54
Group of Seven, xxiii

Halons, 78
Harmonization, xxiii
Harvesting of oceans, 23–26, 70, 76

Hurricanes, 50
Hydrocarbons, xvii, 41

Iceland, 24
Import licenses, 10
Import restrictions, 30, 31–32, 79–80
Imports, 25, 30
Income, global climate change and, 46–48
India: Antarctica and, 13; global climate change and, 59, 80; ocean seabed and, 22; ozone depletion and, 40
Indonesia, xiv, xxi, 59
"Interim Guide Lines for the Voluntary Regulation of Antarctic Pelagic Sealing," 14
International community, 10, 63–64, 70
International Development Agency (IDA), 58, 64
International Energy Agency (IEA), 7
International Geophysical Year, 12
International Monetary Fund (IMF), xiv, xxiii
International Seabed Authority (ISA), 21
International Telecommunications Union (ITU), 18, 19
International Whaling Commission (IWC), 14, 23, 24
Iraq, 2
Italy: Antarctica and, 13; ocean seabed and, 21

Japan, xiv, xvi, xxi, 36, 38, 78; Antarctica and, 13, 14; global climate change and, 56; ocean harvesting and, 23, 24; ocean seabed and, 21, 22; outer space and, 20
Joint management. *See* Collective management

Kennedy Round, xiii
Kerosene, 4, 5
Koomey, Jonathan, 45